How To Fish in Salt Water

How To Fish in Salt Water

by Vlad Evanoff

NEW YORK: A. S. BARNES AND COMPANY, INC.
LONDON: THOMAS YOSELOFF LTD.

Printed in the United States of America

FOREWORD

Success in salt-water fishing depends on many factors which all play a part in the final result. Fishing tackle, lures, baits and other equipment used all have a bearing on the ultimate success or failure of a fishing trip. The author feels that the methods and techniques used in salt-water fishing are also very important, yet they are often neglected, overlooked or unknown to many salt-water anglers. After all, it's a simple matter to go into a well-equipped fishing-tackle store and get a rod, reel, line, lure or bait which will catch fish. But the secret of using this equipment is the key to successful salt-water fishing.

So while this book does include sections on fishing tackle, lures and baits, the main emphasis is on the lesser-known methods, techniques and tricks used by the most experienced salt-water anglers. This know-how usually takes years to acquire the hard way—picking it up bit by bit as you spend many hours bottom fishing, drifting, trolling or casting in the ocean. However, by owning this book, you will have all this information at your finger tips whenever you need it.

Some of the material in this book appeared earlier in the leading outdoor and fishing magazines in the country, which means that several editors selected and bought these articles for their magazines. They felt that they were helpful to their readers. The other sections were written especially for this book. The combination of this material, the author feels, results in one of the best books he has written to date. After you have read this book, I hope you will feel the same way and that it will help you to have more fun and catch more fish in salt water.

VLAD EVANOFF

ACKNOWLEDGMENTS

The author wishes to thank the editors of *Field & Stream, Fishing World, Boating Year Round, Salt-Water Sportsman* and *Sports Afield* magazines for permission to use material which appeared in their publications.

He wishes also to thank the following companies and organizations for supplying photos which were used in this book: Bradlow, Inc., True Temper Corp., South Bend Tackle Co., George Hine Products, The Garcia Corp., Penn Fishing Tackle Mfg. Co., E. I. du Pont de Nemours & Co., Johnson Motors Co., Canadian Government Travel Bureau, Florida State News Bureau, Miami News Bureau, Massachusetts Dept. of Commerce, Delaware State Development Dept., North Carolina News Bureau and Continental Arms Co.

CONTENTS

How To Fish
in Salt Water

1

WHICH FISHING TACKLE FOR YOU?

The average person who first takes up salt-water fishing seriously is usually a pretty confused individual. He sees so many rods, reels, lures and lines in a fishing-tackle store that he becomes bewildered. Which salt-water fishing outfit is the best and which one should he choose for the fishing he wants to do?

Through the years I have recommended fishing outfits for many salt-water fishing novices. I have found that many of them approach the sport with the mistaken notion that *one* outfit can be used for *all* their salt-water fishing. This, of course, is not true and that is why you will find a wide variety of rods, reels and lines being made and sold for salt-water fishing.

However, if you know in advance what type of fishing you like best to do, you will be in a better position to choose the proper outfit for such angling. For example, will most of your fishing be done on the bottom of the sea, with bait and from boats, bridges, piers or the shore? If so, then a salt-water bottom-fishing rod and reel will be the most practical and effective for this type of fishing.

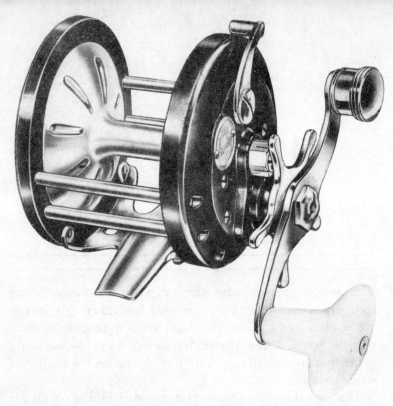

For bottom fishing a boat, bay or pier reel such as this Ocean City reel is ideal.

Salt-water bottom rods usually come in one or two pieces and are often called "boat" rods or "pier" rods. The shorter, lighter ones are also called "weakfish" and "flounder" or "bay" rods. Most bottom-fishing rods run from 5 to 7 ft. in over-all length. Shorter, lighter rods are best when the fish are small, the water shallow and the currents not too strong to make light sinkers impractical. Heavier, longer and stiffer rods are used for the bigger fish, deep water and in strong currents where more lead is needed.

The reels designed for bottom fishing suit the rods being used. For boat and bay rods, reels holding 100 to 300 yds. of line should be used, depending on the type of fishing being done. When you are after small fish in shallow waters and you are using a light rod, the smaller salt-water reels are best. For big fish, deep waters and heavy rods the larger reels are used.

Monofilament lines testing from 15 to 50 lbs. are usually used in bottom fishing with the rods and reels mentioned above. Some anglers also use linen lines, braided-nylon and dacron lines, but for all-around bottom fishing you can't beat the strong, invisible monofilament lines.

If you plan to go after smaller game fish by casting with lures from a boat or the shore, there is one outfit that is almost a must. This is a light salt-water spinning rod which is not too heavy to cast with one hand. The rod should be anywhere from 6 to 7½ ft. in over-all length, and it should

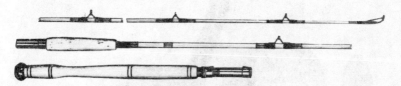

A South Bend Sea Master boat-and-bay bottom-fishing rod.

A light salt-water spinning rod which can be cast with one hand is a versatile tool. This is a Montague 2-piece 7-ft. hollow glass rod.

have enough power and backbone to handle lures up to $1\frac{1}{2}$ oz. in weight. On the other hand, it should have a tip limber enough to cast lures going less than an ounce. Such a rod is used both with heavier or larger fresh-water spinning reels and lighter salt-water types. The best line for this outfit is a monofilament testing 8, 10 or 12 lbs. With such a light spinning outfit you can cast plugs, spoons, jigs and other lures in the North for such fish as striped bass, bluefish and weakfish. In the South it can be used for a wide variety of species, such as snook, sea trout, small tarpon, bonefish, small barracuda, snappers and other fish of similar weights. You can also use

The Garcia Mitchell 306 is a popular salt-water spinning reel used with a one-handed light spinning rod.

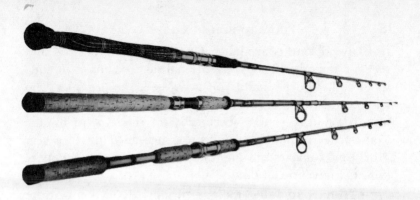

There are spinning rods for pier, bay, boat and surf fishing in salt water. These are Garcia Companion rods.

this outfit with very light sinkers while bottom fishing for small fish.

Another good salt-water spinning outfit which can be used for a wide variety of fishing is the so-called medium-weight spinning rod. This usually runs anywhere from 7½ to 10 ft. in over-all length and has a butt or handle from 14 to 24 in. long. Such a rod is usually cast with two hands. In the shorter lengths it can be used from boats for casting heavier lures. In the longer lengths it can be used for casting from bridges, piers and the shore. Such a rod will cast the heavier lures going up to 2 or 3 oz. The medium-weight spinning outfit can also be used for bottom fishing for smaller species in shallow water and with the lighter sinkers going from 2 to 6 oz. The larger salt-water spinning reels holding anywhere from 150 to 300 yds. of monofilament line testing from 15 to 30 lbs. are used with the rods mentioned above. With medium-weight spinning outfits you can catch many game fish and bottom fish going up to 50 lbs. or so in both northern and southern waters.

When it comes to choosing surf-fishing tackle there are

two kind of outfits available. One is the spinning rod and reel and the other is the conventional surf rod and revolving-spool reel. Which should you get? Well, the beginner who has never used any surf-fishing tackle is better off with a spinning rod and reel made specifically for this type of fishing. You can learn how to cast and use such an outfit in a very short time compared to the time it takes to master the more difficult conventional outfit.

Surf-fishing spinning rods are usually divided into three classes: light, medium and heavy. The light rods range from 7½ to 9½ ft. and handle lures up to about 2 oz. They are usually used with monofilament lines testing about 10 or 12 lbs. In the surf, this is a good outfit for catching small fish such as school striped bass, bluefish, weakfish, whiting or king-fish and croakers.

The medium-weight surf spinning rod runs from about 8 to 10 ft. in over-all length. This rod will generally handle lures ranging from 1 to 4 oz. in weight. It is used with lines testing anywhere from 12 to 20 lbs. If you can afford only one surf spinning rod this is the one to get. It is the nearest thing to an all-around surf-fishing rig and can handle most of the fish found in surf.

Finally, we have the heavyweight surf spinning rod which may run from 9 to 12 ft. or longer in over-all length. Such a heavy rod will handle almost any lure made for surf casting as well as heavy sinkers for bottom fishing. It is used with lines testing from 20 to 30 lbs. or heavier. If you plan to do a lot of bait fishing on the bottom, this is the best outfit to use, especially for big striped bass or channel bass. It is also a favorite with anglers in Cape Cod, Massachusetts, in Rhode Island, in Montauk, New York, and in North Carolina where long casts may be required to reach the fish. However, because of the length and weight of such a rod equipped with

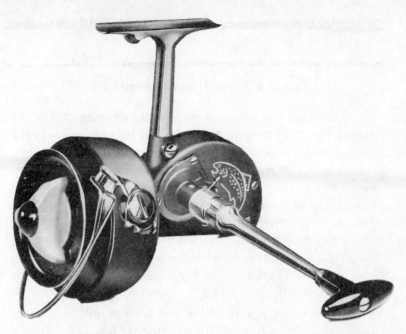

A large spinning reel for surf fishing like this Quick Super is used with a surf spinning rod. It should hold at least 200 yds. of 20-lb. test line. This reel holds 260 yds.

a big reel, casting soon becomes tiring. So, unless you are a big 6-footer built like a wrestler, you will probably find that a medium-weight outfit suits you better for day-in and day-out fishing.

The spinning reels used with surf spinning rods mentioned above will vary in size and weight according to the rod used. For lighter rods and lines you can use the smaller salt-water reels, while the bigger, heavier rods and lines call for the largest spinning reels.

After you have used a surf spinning outfit and find that it is not suitable for some areas and types of surf fishing, you may want to invest in a conventional surf-fishing outfit.

This is a Harnell conventional surf rod.

These rods are also divided into light, medium and heavy classes. The light rods may be only 8 ft. long while the heaviest conventional surf rods may run up to 12 ft. or longer. Here again, the length and weight you use will depend on where you fish, the weight of the lures you cast and the fish you expect to catch. As a general rule, the lighter, shorter rods are best for light lures, short casts and small fish. They are also best for fishing from jetties or breakwaters. The longer, heavier rods are preferable for heavy lures, long casts and big fish. They are best for areas where long casts are necessary and the fish run big.

The conventional surf-fishing reel usually holds anywhere from 150 to 300 yds. of 36-lb. test line. It has a star drag, a free spool, a fast gear ratio and a light, wide spool. The smaller models are used with shorter, lighter rods, while the larger reels are used with longer, heavier surf rods.

Although the modern conventional surf-fishing reel has been perfected through the years and is capable of long casts, you must still practice to master it. Until you educate your thumb to control the revolving spool you'll have trouble with backlashes or "bird's-nests." Some of the reels have anti-backlash devices, which help somewhat, but there's nothing like an educated thumb to guarantee smooth casts.

If you plan to do any offshore fishing you will need special tackle. If you charter a boat, the captain usually supplies the tackle and you don't have to invest in a rod, reel or line. But if you fish from either your own boat or a friend's craft you will need your own tackle. Although offshore-fishing gear can be expensive, there are also rods, reels and accessories on the market which are moderate in price but which do the job.

Today, offshore tackle is usually divided into four classes: light, medium, heavy and extra-heavy. Light rods are used with lines testing anywhere from 12 to 30 lbs. or with 3-thread, 6-thread and 9-thread linen lines. They have a flexible action for use with such light lines. Such a rod is best for smaller offshore fish such as bluefish, bonito, albacore, dolphin, barracuda, king mackerel and similar fish that weigh up to 50 lbs. or so. Incidentally, this tackle can also be used for striped-bass and channel-bass trolling.

The Penn Squidder is a typical conventional-type surf-fishing reel with a wide light-plastic spool, star drag and free spool.

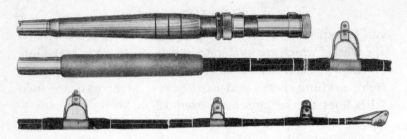

The Harnell offshore or big-game rod comes in different actions and weights.

The medium-weight rods for offshore fishing should be used with lines testing from 30 to 70 lbs. or with linen lines of 12, 15, 18 or 21 threads. Such rods are best for sailfish, white marlin, striped marlin, school tuna, wahoo, amberjack and similar fish ranging from 50 to 300 lbs. in weight.

Heavy offshore rods should be used with lines testing from 70 to 130 lbs. or linen lines of 24, 36 and 39 threads. Such rods are used for bigger fish such as blue marlin, swordfish, giant tuna and sharks. Fish ranging from 300 to 1,000 lbs. are sought with this gear.

Extra-heavy offshore rods are the work horses which are reserved for the biggest game fish found in the ocean. They are used with lines testing from 130 to 180 lbs. Such tackle should only be used when you are seeking swordfish, blue marlin, black marlin, giant tuna and sharks weighing 1,000 lbs. and up. It should also be used when fishing conditions call for the heaviest lines and rods.

When it comes to reels for offshore fishing you will find different sizes to match the rods and lines used. Reels No. 1/0, 2/0, 3/0 and 4/0, for example, are used with light rods and lines. For medium rods and lines you should use No. 6/0 and 9/0 reels. For heavy tackle the No. 10/0, 12/0 and 14/0 reels are used. While for the extra-heavy tackle you may need the No. 16/0 job at times. Reels are made for off-shore fishing in moderately priced ranges from $20.00 to $150.00 or expensive models ranging from $250.00 to $650.00. These reels are filled with either dacron or linen lines made especially for big-game fishing.

If you live in Florida or fish the Gulf of Mexico you may want to get a "popping" rod, which is similar to a fresh-water bait-casting rod but somewhat longer and heavier. Such rods run from 6 to 7½ ft. in over-all length and are used with special bait-casting reels made for salt water. These usually have star drags and free spools and are heavier and

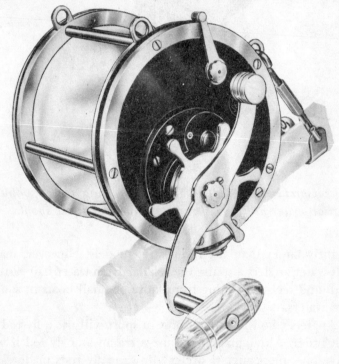

The Penn Senator offshore or big-game reel comes in many sizes.

The Garcia Ambassadeur 5000 bait-casting reel is popular for salt-water fishing. It has a star drag and a free spool.

slightly larger than the fresh-water models. However, many salt-water anglers also use the regular fresh-water bait-casting rods and reels for fishing from shore or small boats in southern waters.

Anglers who want the utmost in sport will use a fly rod in salt water. Although you can use a fresh-water fly rod if you have one, most anglers prefer salt-water fly rods made especially for salt-water fishing. The rod itself may run from 8 to 9½ ft. in over-all length. Shorter rods are preferred for fish which can be caught with short casts, just as longer rods are best where longer casts are often necessary.

The reels used for salt-water fly fishing are similar to those used for salmon fishing in fresh water. In fact, many of the well-made salmon reels can be used in fishing for striped bass, channel bass, weakfish, snook and small tarpon. But if you go after bonefish or big tarpon you may want a special salt-water fly reel holding the fly line in addition to at least 200 to 300 yds. of backing line.

Most salt-water rods today are made from hollow glass blanks, and these are usually the best for most fishing. However, solid-glass rods are often used for bottom fishing and trolling. Some big-game rods are made from laminated woods, and fly rods are still made from split bamboo for the minority of anglers who prefer them. But the average angler will find that the hollow fiber-glass rods offer the best value and are the most durable.

You can get a pretty good idea of the type of rod you need from the preceding discussion. However, to make sure, you can ask the advice of a friend who does the type of fishing you plan to do. He can usually recommend an outfit similar to the one he uses or even suggest a better one. Fishing-tackle dealers who have their stores located near your fishing area can often recommend the best outfit for you and for the fishing you plan to do. But you have to give them some information to go on in making the selection. In order to do this try to narrow down the type of fishing to the one you will be doing *most* of the time. When you have this information firmly in mind you can make a wise selection and get a salt-water outfit which will perform best.

2

USING SALT-WATER LURES

When I first started fishing in salt water about twenty-five years ago, very few anglers used artificial lures. Most of them depended on natural baits when they went fishing in the ocean. The handful of anglers who used artificial lures at that time didn't have many to choose from. They used mostly metal squids, cedar and bone jigs and feather lures.

Today the picture has changed and tackle manufacturers are turning out a wide variety of salt-water lures. Salt-water fishermen are using metal squids, jigs, spoons, spinners, plugs, flies, eelskin lures, rigged eels and rubber and plastic lures. Many salt-water anglers now carry a good assortment of these lures when they go out fishing.

Yet mere possession of a wide assortment of salt-water fishing lures is no guarantee of fishing success. You also have to know which lures to use at a given time and how to use them. The most successful salt-water anglers know not only which lures to use and which sizes, weights and colors are best, but also how to manipulate the particular lure to provoke the most strikes from the fish. So it pays to make a thorough study of the various salt-water lures and how they can be used most effectively.

One of the oldest artificial lures used in surf fishing is the metal squid, which is also used in casting and trolling from a boat. Through the years, metal squids have changed little and they are still great fish-getters when used properly and at the right time. There are many different kinds of metal squids on the market, and these vary in shape, size and weight. Most of them imitate such broad or flat fish as mullet, sardines and herring, or they try to imitate such long, slim bait fish as sand eels and silversides or spearing. The best metal squids are made of block tin which can be polished with fine steel wool. They can also be bent to form a slight curve, which gives them more action in the water.

The best metal squid is nothing more than a chunk of metal with a hook and feathers or bucktail. But they won't catch fish unless they are made to look alive and irresistible. To the casual observer watching an expert surf angler using a metal squid, it looks easy. But it is more complicated than it appears. The wind, current, tide and waves in the surf all work against the angler in his attempts to give the lure a lifelike action. Still, the metal squid is one of the most effective lures to use in surf when the water is rough and white.

The secret to getting the best action out of a metal squid in the surf is to wait until a wave breaks, then to cast your squid behind it. If you don't the incoming wave will pick up your squid and bring it toward you faster than you can take up the slack. A slack line will stop the action of your squid and cause it to sink.

On the other hand, after a wave breaks, the water rushes back out to sea, creating a pull against your lure. In this case you have to slow your reeling, since reeling fast at this time will cause your squid to spin and rise to the surface. The same thing holds true in a strong current—you have to reel slowly to get the best action out of a squid, for a fast current or tide will give the squid the proper action even if you barely turn the handle of the reel. After a while you will

The correct choice of lure is important, but knowing how to use it is even more important if you want to get results.

develop a certain "feel" for the properly working squid, and you will be able to change the speed of the retrieve to suit the waves and water encountered.

When the fish are on the surface of the water chasing bait fish, you have to reel your squid fairly fast to keep it near the top. Holding the tip of your rod high also helps. When the fish are not showing or when they are not hitting a fast-moving squid near the surface, you can try reeling slowly and allowing the squid to sink. In fact, there are times when striped bass and weakfish prefer a metal squid which is barely moving. Weakfish, especially, will often hit a light metal squid when it is sinking toward the bottom. In order to get this effect, you should cast out and, as the squid sinks, just turn the reel handle enough to keep a taut line. The squid will have plenty of action as it flutters toward the bottom. Of course, when it does reach the bottom, you will have to reel faster to keep it moving and prevent it from resting there.

The metal squid is mostly used in surf fishing, but it is also sometimes deadly when cast or trolled from a boat. Under these conditions, it will take such fish as bluefish, striped bass, bonito, albacore, weakfish, mackerel and pollock.

The speed at which you reel or troll your metal squid is an important factor when you are seeking certain species of fish. Striped bass usually hit a fast-moving squid that is fished over rocky bottoms such as those found at Montauk, New York, and in Rhode Island. Over sandy bottoms, reeling at a moderate speed is best. Smaller striped bass usually prefer a faster moving metal squid than big stripers. In fact, most of the stripers caught on metal squids are the smaller school fish. Big cow stripers are only occasionally caught on metal squids, usually during a slow or moderate retrieve.

Other fish that like a fast-moving metal squid are bluefish, bonito, albacore and mackerel. For some of these fish, such as the bonito or albacore, you have to reel in as fast as you can turn the handle of the reel, or troll anywhere from 6 to 10 m.p.h. with a boat.

Among the fish that prefer a slow-moving metal squid are

weakfish, channel bass and pollock. If you reel very slowly you will sometimes even catch fluke or summer flounders on metal squids.

Metal squids are used with feathers or bucktail tied around the hook. The most effective colors are usually white, yellow, red or combinations of these. A strip of pork rind added to the bare hook of a metal squid is also highly effective.

Another "old-time" lure used in salt water is the spoon. There are now many sizes and shapes on the market. The ones made for salt-water use are usually nickel or chrome plated or made of stainless steel. A few of the smaller spoons are equipped with treble hooks, but for the greatest strength large single hooks are usually used. The smaller spoons are ideal for casting with a spinning outfit. The larger ones are preferable for trolling.

Most salt-water game fish that feed on smaller fish will strike a spoon. Its wobbling action and bright flash will attract fish in most waters. When using smaller spoons with a spinning or bait-casting outfit a slow or moderate retrieve is best. The minute you feel the spoon working on the end of the line, maintain that speed. As you reel, jerk the rod tip to make the spoon dart forward and rise, then drop the rod tip and make a few turns. This causes the spoon to rise, then flutter and sink, thus imitating a crippled, helpless bait fish. Such fish as striped bass, channel bass, snook, tarpon, weakfish and many others will go for it.

When trolling from a boat, a slow or moderate speed is also best when using spoons. Here it is important to find the depth at which the fish are feeding. As a general rule such fish as striped bass, bluefish, channel bass, tarpon, albacore, bonito and king mackerel will hit spoons trolled near the surface. This is especially true when they are chasing bait fish. However, there are times when you have to go deeper for them. Then you must attach weights and trolling sinkers above the spoon or use wire or lead-core lines.

In recent years large spoons up to 12 in. long equipped with husky 10/0 or 12/0 hooks have been used to catch big striped bass. These spoons, called "bunker" spoons, imitate such large bait fish as menhaden or herring and are killers during the spring and fall runs of big stripers off New Jersey, Long Island, New York, Rhode Island and Massachusetts. Channel bass and big bluefish also have been taken on these large spoons.

Some of these big spoons come attached to lead keels, which can be adjusted to control both the depth at which the lure travels and its action. For best results big spoons should be made to sway and wobble from side to side and should not spin or revolve. The boat should troll as slowly as possible or just fast enough to bring about this action.

Spinners are also good lures to use when trolling, especially for the smaller fish found in bays, inlets and rivers. Nickel-plated, chrome-plated and stainless-steel spinners are most suitable for salt-water use. The blades can be oval, round or leaf-shaped. The narrow willow-leaf-type spinners are very popular. Although spinners will catch fish when used alone, they are usually used with feather or bucktail

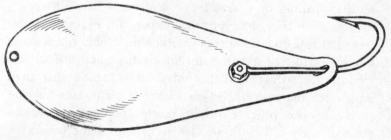

A bunker spoon

hooks or in combination with various baits, such as sea worms, strips of squid, pork rind or small whole bait fish.

The spinner, such as the Cape Cod type, with bloodworms or sandworms on a gang hook behind it is a consistent catcher of school stripers. For best results spinners should be trolled deep and slowly with at least 75 to 100 ft. of line out. The so-called fluke spinner consists of two blades and is used with small bait fish such as killies or spearing on the hook. The spinner is attached above a sinker and is bounced off the bottom while drifting in a boat.

Turning to plugs we encounter a form of lure which offers some of the finest sport in salt-water fishing. There is no greater thrill than seeing a big striper, bluefish, tarpon, sea trout or other salt-water game fish come up and take a whack at a surface plug. Salt-water anglers will now find on the market a wide variety of plugs made of wood or plastic. These surface-type plugs come in sizes that vary from 3-in. models for light spinning to big, heavy 12-in. plugs suitable only for heavy surf outfits or for trolling.

Surface plugs include types called poppers, torpedo-shapes and swimmers as well as types which have propellers or revolving tails. Most of them are designed to create a ripple, spray or splash on top of the water in order to attract fish. The secret in using these lures is to make them simulate crippled or sluggish bait fish such as menhaden, herring, mullet, sardines or silversides or a terrified bait fish trying to escape the jaws of larger fish. Poppers, for example, when jerked, throw up a big spray of water which looks like a game fish in pursuit of a bait fish. No doubt, game fish in the vicinity are attracted to this splash and, feeling that they must catch the bait fish before other fish get it, take a swipe at the surface plug. For best results, poppers should be worked fairly fast with regular jerks and slight pauses in between.

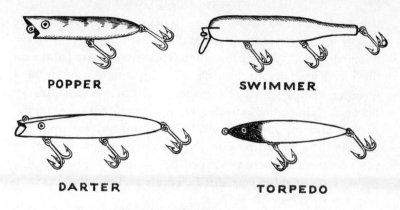

POPPER

SWIMMER

DARTER

TORPEDO

Popular salt-water plugs

The torpedo-shaped surface plugs are deadly lures in southern waters. They are favorite lures in Florida for such fish as tarpon, snook, sea trout, jack crevallé and other surface feeders. They, too, should be worked rapidly on top with long sweeps or jerks of the rod tip to make it skip along the surface.

Another surface plug is the swimming type which usually has a metal lip, a good example being the Striper Atom. When reeled fast and jerked, this lure can also be made to throw up a big splash like a popper. When used in this manner it is very effective for big striped bass. At other times it should be reeled slowly or at a moderate speed so that it will swim on top with a snakelike action creating a wake or ripple behind it. Some plugs of this type come in long, double-jointed models and resemble eels or big bait fish floundering on top of the water.

Another plug which is not exactly a surface model since it rides a few inches below when reeled fast is the darter type. This was long a favorite in fresh water and has been widely used for snook, tarpon and sea trout in Florida waters. Now larger and stronger types have become popular in surf fishing for striped bass and bluefish. Darter plugs have notched heads, which cause them to swim or dart from side to side. Especially in Florida, they are often worked in a series of snappy whips of the rod, with fairly fast reeling in between. This plug can also be worked alternately on the surface and just below it by holding the rod tip up, then lowering it and reeling fast. Surf anglers also use the darter plug on top for catching striped bass at night. They do this by working the plug very slowly, barely reeling in and twitching it as it lies on the surface.

Underwater plugs may or may not float when at rest. Some do, and then dive to varying depths on the retrieve. Others sink immediately and either dive even deeper or travel on the same level when reeled in or trolled. These plugs usually have metal lips or heads cut at an angle, both to make them dive and to give them action—usually a dart or side-to-side wriggle. However, some plugs are blunt or pointed and have little or no built-in action. These must be worked with the rod tip to give them a lifelike look.

When using underwater plugs, you must get a certain feel which travels up the line and indicates that the plug is working properly. The key to accomplishing this is to change the speed of the retrieve so that you always feel the plug working. When the tide or a wave pushes the plug in your direction, you will have to speed up the retrieve, and if the current or backwash pulls the plug away from you, then you must slow down your reeling. As a general rule, clear, calm water calls for somewhat faster reeling to produce strikes than is necessary when fishing in rough or dirty water. Likewise, daytime fishing calls for a faster retrieve than night-time fishing.

Although most underwater plugs have a built-in wriggle, they are often better producers if they are jerked at intervals, stopped or slowed down, then speeded up to create an erratic action.

When using either surface or underwater plugs in such areas as narrow tidal creeks or rivers in Florida, along rocky shores and around piles bridges or other obstructions, it is important to cast the plug accuately. The same is true when you see fish such as bonefish, tarpon, snook or channel bass in low, clear water. Under such conditions a plug which lands in the right spot will often be hit, but if it is off by a few feet it may fail to bring a strike or, worse yet, frighten the fish away.

If there is any salt-water lure which can be called an all-around fish getter it is the jig. It is one of the deadliest fishing lures made when in the hands of a man who knows how to use it. These lures have heavy heads, made of lead or other metal and feathers, bucktail, nylon or plastic skirts wrapped around the hook. The metal head is plated, chromed or painted in various colors. Those with white, yellow or red hair, feathers or combinations of these are used most frequently.

In recent years jigs have become very popular, especially with spin casters. However, they are really old-time lures and the famed Japanese feather jig has been used both abroad and in this country for many years. It is still a top lure for trolling behind a boat and will take tuna, bluefish, bonito, albacore, mackerel and similar surface feeders.

The smaller jigs ranging from 1/8 to 1 1/2 oz. are the most popular. It is amazing how many different kinds of fish can be caught on jigs. Almost every kind of game fish and many so-called bottom fish will hit these lures. Some anglers fishing in southern waters have caught over one hundred different species of fish on jigs.

Jigs are also highly versatile lures and can be trolled, cast or bounced on the bottom. When such fish as striped bass,

When fishing for bonito you must reel or troll a lure fast if you want to get strikes.

bluefish, tuna, albacore, bonito, mackerel or barracuda are feeding on the surface, a jig trolled fast or cast and reeled at a good speed will often take them.

Another technique for using the jig is to cast it out, allow it to sink a few feet, jerk it, allow it to sink again, then jerk it again and so on. I have used a variation of this successfully for bonito and albacore when these fish refused the regular butterfish or menhaden bait on a hook. The fish showed up in the chum slick and could be seen darting at chunks of the bunker. So we tried dropping back white bucktail jigs with silver heads and working them up and down quickly in the chum. The albacore and bonito would grab these at regular intervals.

The jig is one of the few lures which can get down deep in a strong current and which is highly effective in canals, rivers and tidal rips. Here you cast upstream or up the current and let the jig drift and sink with the tide. If the current is very strong you can let out slack line to permit the lure to sink still deeper. When the jig hits bottom you should start reeling back with regular jerks. Most strikes will occur when the jig leaves the bottom on its way up.

Another way to use jigs when drifting or anchored in a boat is to let the jig down to the bottom, make it dance up and down by jerking the rod tip up, and then let the jig settle again. Keep repeating this process until a strike occurs. When doing this you will hook many so-called bottom fish which are rarely taken on other artificial lures.

Salt-water anglers looking for the ultimate in sport use a fly rod for many of the smaller species. Streamers, bucktails and popper bugs are the main types of lures used in this type of fishing. Surface-feeding fish such as striped bass, bluefish, snook, sea trout and small tarpon go for the popper bugs especially when the water is fairly calm or when they are chasing small bait fish. For best results the popper bugs should be jerked hard to create a lot of commotion. Streamers and bucktails are retrieved in foot-long jerks punctuated by pauses either near the surface or down deep. Near the surface these lures will take almost any game fish that hits artificials. Down deep they will catch not only game fish, but also many bottom species.

Then there are such natural baits as rigged eels and eelskin lures which are used like artificials. The rigged eel is a great lure when you are casting from the surf or a boat for big striped bass. It is most effective for stripers at night when it is reeled very slowly with occasional jerks of the rod tip. Rigged eels can also be used for trolling on the surface for such fish as white marlin. They can also be equipped with weights and trolled deep in tidal rips for big bluefish.

Eelskin lures are used for striped bass and bluefish in casting and trolling. You can work them near the surface by reeling or trolling fast or near the bottom by working them slowly. Surf anglers fishing fast currents, such as those in Cape Cod Canal, like to work their eelskin lures with continual jerks in order to imitate the stop-and-go movement of the natural squid. When trolling, it is also a good idea to jerk the rod tip at regular intervals.

Finally, we have such lures as the rubber surgical tube and the plastic tube. In these lures, the hook is run through the hole in the tube so that one end of it rests against the bend of the hook. When trolled, these lures leave a trail of bubbles and have a twisting action which is especially effective for bluefish but which will also catch striped bass, albacore, bonito and other fish.

There are also quite a few rubber lures on the market which are made to imitate natural baits such as sea worms, squid, eels, shrimp and bait fish. Many of these lures look and feel like real creatures. These lures usually have no built-in action, so it is up to the angler to provide the movement which produces strikes.

Actually, the real reason why one angler may catch more fish than another with the same lures is that the successful man knows the technique for using his lures. The man who will catch the most fish will be the angler who hits on the right combination of depth, reeling or trolling speed and rod manipulation. It pays to experiment until you find the perfect combination.

3

LOCATING FISH IN THE SURF

One of the toughest problems confronting the novice in surf fishing is the one of locating the fish that venture inshore to feed. As the beginner glances up and down the miles of beach, he is likely to scratch his head and wonder where he should cast his lure or bait. To him, one section of breaking waves and water looks very much like any other, and he finds it difficult to choose the best spot for fishing.

The veteran surf angler, on the other hand, can study the water and surf, then head for a certain spot where his chances of catching fish are good. How does he do it? Well, most experienced surf anglers have the ability to "read" the surf and water. By studying the way the waves break, the color of the water and the characteristics of the tides and rips, they obtain clues to the best fishing spots which are overlooked by the beginner. Veteran surf anglers have also developed their powers of observation to the point where they are able to notice every little movement or indication of feeding fish.

Unfortunately for the newcomer, however, this ability to choose the best fishing spots in the surf takes time to acquire. Through years of trial and error the seasoned surf anglers have learned which spots are the most productive and which ones to ignore. But the beginner may spend hours fishing a barren spot. What to do about it?

Well, even veteran surf anglers can't catch fish in the surf unless the quarry is there. So most surf anglers wait until they hear that the fish are running at a certain beach before they go out at all. The outdoor-column writers of the daily newspapers in coastal areas often print information about local runs of surf fish. This data can serve as a guide to the best general fishing spots. But, since it is usually a day or two late, this news may have lost much of its value by the time it gets printed. Hence the rule: If you read about a run of fish at a nearby beach, try to get there the same day, if possible. If you wait a day or two, the action may have migrated elsewhere or the fish may have stopped feeding.

However, even if you can't manage to go fishing on such short notice, it is still of some value to make a mental note of the spot and try it when you do get a chance to go out. Schools of fish usually stay in a general area for days or weeks and may start feeding again at any time.

You can also obtain information on the hot surf-fishing spots from friends and fishing-tackle dealers. If you have a surf-fishing buddy make a mutual agreement to keep each other informed when and where you catch fish in the surf. Or drop around to the local fishing-tackle store and talk to either the owner or surf anglers who have been out fishing. Many surf anglers come into the local store to weigh a big fish or buy a lure or line. The dealer gets a good idea of the spots that are producing fish and is glad to pass this information on to his customers.

The beginning surf fisherman often has a favorite way of locating the best fishing spots. He goes down to the beach and looks for other anglers. If he sees a line of surf anglers he joins them in the belief that they are fishing the best

Surf anglers often spend hours traveling around and scanning the waters for signs of fish.

spot. This may or may not be true. If the anglers are catching fish or have caught fish at that spot recently then it's a good idea to join them. But if no fish are being caught you may be wasting your time fishing there. You can often do better by finding a less crowded spot. In fact, even if a few fish *are* being caught at the time you can still increase your chances by trying a different location where there is less competition.

Surf fish such as striped bass, bluefish, channel bass, weakfish and others often move fast. They may be present and active in a certain area and then, in a matter of minutes, disappear. So when these species are moving in large schools and actively feeding on smaller bait fish, the best way to locate them is to look for birds, especially gulls and terns, diving and wheeling over the water. This usually indicates that larger game fish down below are driving the bait fish to the surface.

When the birds are within casting distance, it's always a good idea to cast a metal squid or surface plug into the commotion. If there are big fish feeding, the chances are good that you will get a strike. But even if the birds are outside of casting range or merely sitting on the water, it pays to keep an eye on them. If the bait fish move in to shore, the birds and game fish will follow and you'll often be able to reach them. On many occasions, I've spent many hours during the day watching gulls and terns wheeling and diving too far offshore to reach with a cast. However, toward dusk, the bait fish often headed inshore and then there would be fast action as the bigger fish followed them right up to the beach.

Sometimes you don't see any birds working, but you will either see small bait fish skipping or leaping out of the water or you will see a big fish slap the water with its tail or swirl as it chases a smaller fish. In either case it's an indication that fish are present and feeding. Then it's up to you to find the lure that they want.

So far we've covered the easy ways to locate fish in the surf. Now, how about the days when there are no anglers catching fish, no birds, and no bait fish or other signs of game fish? How do you locate fish at such times?

This is when the ability to read the water and shore formations pays off big for the veteran surf angler. Naturally, the local anglers who fish a certain area often have a big advantage when it comes to choosing the best fishing spots. They know from past experience which spots have produced under varying conditions of weather, wind, tides and seasons. So they head for these spots when the same conditions arise and connect more often than a stranger fishing the area for the first time.

However, there are many general rules and signs that reveal the best fishing spots—provided you know what to look for. Take the color of the water, for example. This can reveal the location of deep or shallow spots. The presence of dark blue, dark green or green water is a sign that the water is deep and can pinpoint a hole, slough or channel. These are all good spots to try.

Light green, brownish or white water, on the other hand, reveals a shallow spot and the presence of a reef, sand or rock bar, or flats. When there are bait fish present in these shallow areas and the water is moderately rough, such shallow spots often provide good fishing for striped bass.

The way the waves break on shore also indicates the depth and type of bottom found in the area. The breaking of waves some distance offshore usually reveals a sand or rock bar or a gently sloping beach. Here you will often have to cast beyond the breakers to catch fish. If you can wade out on the sand bar or into the water some distance you stand a better chance of catching fish.

On the other hand, when the waves approach close to shore before they curl and break, it usually indicates a sharply sloping beach where you can often catch such fish as striped bass, channel bass, bluefish and weakfish close to shore.

Along sand beaches you will often find a sand bar well offshore and deeper water closer to the beach. Such holes and sloughs often contain surf fish, especially at the high tides and half tides. The fish like to lie just inside the outer sand bar and wait for food to be washed out or for bait fish to swim past. In such spots it's a good idea to cast your lure on the sand bar and reel it into the deeper water.

Sand bars rarely continue unbroken when they run parallel to a beach. Usually there are channels and cuts which allow the water to enter and leave, and these spots have deeper water and stronger currents and rips. Such marine life as crabs, sand bugs, clams, worms and bait fish get swept into or tossed around in this turmoil and bigger game fish will wait for the easy pickings found there.

Even if you have trouble locating a good fishing spot along a sandy beach there is still one reliable method that can produce fish. It means plenty of casting and walking but you cover a lot of territory and can often run into good fishing. You start working a stretch of beach by merely casting two or three times in one spot, then move about 50 feet down the beach and do the same thing there. To cover the maximum area with this method you should not cast straight into the ocean at each stop. Instead, you make one cast at an angle to your left, the next one straight in front of you and the third cast to your right. Naturally, if you run into a school of fish or start getting strikes you can stop and fish that area thoroughly.

Along rocky bottoms and shores, such as those found in parts of Massachusetts, Rhode Island and Montauk, New York, locating fish can be simple or difficult depending on your knowledge of the area. But good places do not change very often, so once you have taken a fish from a certain location you can often repeat in the future.

The high cliffs found along rocky shores attract many surf anglers because these formations seem to promise good fishing. In practice, however, they are often poor fishing locations. True, they usually have deep water nearby, but you can't get into position to fish it. If you have to stand 30 or 40 feet above the water to fish from a cliff you might as well pass it up. It is just too difficult to work a lure properly or land a big fish from such a height. However, if you can get

Along rocky shores such as those found in parts of Massa-chusetts and Rhode Island and at Montauk, New York, striped bass are often found feeding close to submerged or exposed rocks.

down to a low-lying rock or ledge near such a spot you can often have excellent fishing. With deep water adjacent to the cliff fish venture very close and can be hooked almost at your feet.

Rocky points which jut out into the ocean also provide good surf fishing. If the waves are breaking against the point and creating white water you will often find striped bass feeding here.

Other productive spots along rocky shores include coves, rocks, mussel bars and exposed or submerged boulders. Most coves in such areas contain sunken or exposed rocks and boulders. When the water is rough the waves crashing over these rocks often create foamy white water. Striped bass like to lie in this white foam, on the short side of the obstructions. A lure cast into the boiling brine will bring a quick strike if a fish is present. And you can return to such a spot again and again and catch the stripers that move in to take the place of those caught earlier.

Locating fish in the surf along beaches that have jetties and breakwaters is, of course, simplified by the presence of these structures because you can fish from the jetties or breakwaters themselves. However, all such man-made rock piles aren't equally productive. One jetty or breakwater may be better than another, but only experience and many fishing trips will show which ones produce the most fish.

As a general rule, you will find that the fish you get from a jetty or breakwater depends on the tides. At high tide you can often catch fish close to shore where the jetty begins. Stripers, especially, will be found in the white water close to the beach and also in the wash created by waves breaking on

The ends of jetties and breakwaters are always good spots to try for various kinds of fish.

the sides of the rocks. In fact, striped bass will often lie along-side a jetty, almost at your feet. So, when you reel in your lure, be prepared for a strike even during the last few feet of the retrieve.

The extreme end of a jetty or breakwater offers good fishing on many other occasions—unless the high tide or breaking waves make it difficult to "fish from the far end." The waves breaking in front may force a surf angler to stay back some distance. At such times, to fish in safety he may have to wait until the tide drops or until low tide returns. But enough big striped bass and other surf fish have been caught from the ends of jetties even at low tide to make the wait worthwhile.

One reason why larger jetties and breakwaters provide good fishing is because many of them are built adjacent to an inlet. Smaller fish and bait fish move in and out of the inlet with the tides and attract the larger game fish. In fact, inlets along sandy and rocky shores provide good surf fishing even if there are no jetties or breakwaters. The wise angler always spends as much time as he can fishing at such inlets. Of course, the best time to fish is during the outgoing tide, especially the last two or three hours of it. Then bait fish and other marine life are swept out to sea where the big babies are waiting.

Generally, the best way to locate surf fish is to move around from spot to spot. The angler who stays rooted in one spot and waits for fish to come to him often misses some fast action taking place in other areas. In the surf, conditions are always changing, depending on tides, weather, location of bait fish, etc. One spot may be hot one day and cool off the next. A few miles down the beach, anglers may be hauling in fish while anglers in other areas are catching nothing.

I find it's always a good idea to "case" a stretch of beach or a certain area before actually fishing. This can be done early in the morning or in the afternoon. You can drive around and talk to tackle dealers and other anglers to get the lowdown on the fishing situation. Keep an eye on the water for signs of birds working, fish or bait breaking and fishing boats trolling near shore. (Binoculars are a big help for such observations.) If you see fish being caught or learn that they were caught earlier you have some useful information. The next step is to find out which tide and lures produced the fish. Then all that remains is to return that evening or on the next tide when conditions will be similar.

Locating fish in the surf is not too difficult for the observant angler who plays detective and makes use of every clue that reveals the best fishing.

4

USE THE RIGHT RIG

Every angler who fishes in salt water should be familiar with the various rigs used for casting, trolling and bottom fishing. This terminal tackle has evolved through years and years of experimentation in presenting lures and baits to fish. The rigs vary according to the area being fished, the fish being sought, the tackle being used and the fishing method in use at the time. Rigs play a big part in successful fishing or the lack of it, and the smart anglers soon learn when, where and how to use each rig.

The simplest rig in salt-water fishing is used for still fishing with a cane pole. Here you merely tie a hook on the end of a line or a nylon leader and lower it into the water. Sometimes a float or bobber is attached above the hook. With a shorter leader this rig can also be used with casting tackle. Usually a split-shot or clincher sinker is added above the hook but below the float to keep the baited hook at the proper level in a tide or current.

Any time you are casting with lures in salt water, whether with a light one-handed spinning rod or a heavy conventional surf rod, it's a good idea to use a "shocker" leader. This is a length of nylon material which is tied to the end of the main fishing line. It should be a few pounds stronger than the main line. With spinning tackle this leader should

49

be long enough so that when the lure is reeled in all the way a few turns of it should be left on the reel spool. With conventional tackle the leader can consist of nylon mono-filament long enough to reach almost to the reel spool when the line is reeled all the way in.

Usually a snap can be tied to the end of the leader, and the lure can in turn be attached to this. But if you are fish-ing where there are bluefish, barracuda or other sharp-toothed fish around, a wire leader can be attached to the end of the line or to the lure itself. This should be no more than 6 to 8 in. long when used for casting and 2 or 3 ft. long when trolled with light tackle.

When trolling for larger game fish, you may need leaders up to even 15 ft. in length for many of the larger billfish such as sailfish, marlin, sharks, etc. Two kinds of leader are usually used for this type of salt-water fishing. One is the cable-type leader while the other is the single-strand stain-less-steel wire.

The rigs used for casting and trolling are relatively simple, and the same rig can usually be used in many parts of the country and for different kinds of salt-water fish. But when we come to bottom-fishing rigs we run into a different prob-lem. Here, there are rigs which can be used for many species, but there are also special rigs which are only good for spe-cific fish.

If you are party-boat fishing, ask the mate or a nearby angler for advice on rigging. Ask, too, at bridges, piers or other places where experienced anglers are present. Tackle dealers will also be glad to show you which rigs to use and how to make them. You can also buy ready-made rigs for many kinds of fish, but because these are often too elaborate and expensive, most bottom fishermen prefer to tie their own rigs. Each angler has his own ideas and preferences, and that's part of the fun in bottom fishing.

For your rigs you'll need a few supplies, such as swivels, wire leaders, sinkers and hooks. Start with some three-way swivels of various sizes. The size 3/0 is about the largest you'll ever need. For light-tackle fishing the small No. 4 swivel is about right. In-between sizes such as the 2/0, 1/0, 1 and 2 swivels should be obtained for use when needed. Some barrel swivels in sizes 3/0, 1/0, 2 and 4 are also good to have on hand.

For making leaders or for snelling hooks, nylon leader material testing 10, 15, 20, 30, 40 and 50 lbs. will be needed for most forms of bottom fishing. These can be obtained in coils of from 10-yd. to 100-yd. lengths. If you are after sharp-toothed fish such as bluefish, barracuda, sharks, etc., you can use cable-wire leader material instead of nylon. Wire leaders are also used for surf fishing for big striped bass, channel bass, sharks and rays.

The most commonly used sinker for bottom fishing is the bank type, although the diamond-shaped style is popular too. In rocky areas, round sinkers are sometimes used, but in surf fishing on sandy bottoms pyramid sinkers hold best. For light tackle and shallow water a 1-oz. or 2-oz. sinker will often serve, but when you are using heavy tackle and thick lines in deep water with strong currents or tides, you may need sinkers up to 12 oz.

Regarding hooks: you can often buy them on short or long leaders in almost any tackle store. If you want to tie or snell your own, loose hooks bought by the dozen or by the box are the best and most economical. Buy them with eyes if you want to tie on the nylon leader material or without eyes if you want to wrap them with fine silk or nylon thread to make snelled hooks. Eyed hooks will save you time and are preferred by most anglers. The hook pattern and size you use depends, of course, on the fish you are after, the tackle you use and where you are fishing. The most

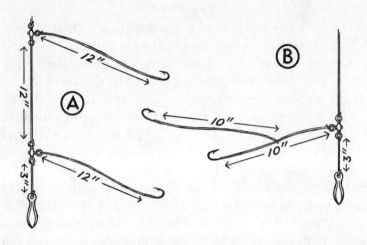

These are basic bottom rigs. "A" illustrates the so-called "deep sea" or "bottom" rig. "B" shows a popular bottom rig for flounders and blackfish.

popular patterns include the O'Shaughnessy, Eagle Claw, Carlisle and Sproat. Special hooks, such as the Virginia, are used for blackfish or tautog. Chestertown hooks are favorites for winter flounder and Sheepshead hooks are used for the sheepshead, a large member of the porgy family.

The basic rig for bottom fishing—one that has been used for many years—consists simply of a snelled hook tied a few inches above the sinker. Some anglers merely tie the loop of the snelled hook into the main line and let it go at that. But often this allows the hook and leader to get wrapped around the main line. A three-way swivel tied on the line allows the hook to clear the main line. Instead of using the three-way swivel, some anglers wrap waterproof tape around the line and leader at the point where the tie is made. This stiffens the section and also forces the hook to swing away from the line. There are also various cross-line swivels and spreaders on the market which do the same thing, but the tendency in recent years has been to get away from as much "hardware" in a rig as possible.

The basic bottom rig is also made up with two or more hooks on the line. The popular "deep-sea" rig makes use of two hooks, one tied just above the sinker and the other just high enough above the first to clear it. This rig is used from party boats fishing the offshore wrecks and banks. It is used with small, short-snelled hooks for blackfish or tautog, sea bass, porgies, whiting, ling and similar fish. With longer leaders and larger hooks it is used for codfish, haddock and pollock. For herring, smelt and a few other fish as many as three or four hooks may be tied on, one above the other.

Another bottom rig which has become increasingly popu-

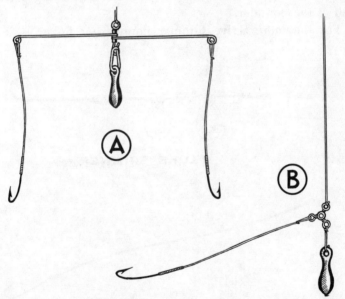

Two types of flounder rigs. "A" illustrates the spreader type with two hooks. "B" shows a single-hook rig attached to a three-way swivel on the line.

lar in recent years consists of a nylon leader about 14 in. in length tied a few inches above the sinker and another hook on a short 8-in. nylon snell tied near the center of the longer 14-in. leader. This creates a two-hook rig which lies right on the bottom and is especially useful for blackfish or tautog, winter flounder and kingfish (northern whiting). It is also good for eels and any other species which picks or sucks its food from the bottom.

A special winter-flounder rig is the type which makes use of a spreader. The sinker is tied in the center of this heavy-wire device and two Chestertown hooks on short snells are attached on the ends. This rig also lies on the bottom, but it is cumbersome and heavy, making it difficult to detect a bite or to get the maximum sport out of playing such a fish as the flounder.

For the more active summer flounder or fluke, as it is

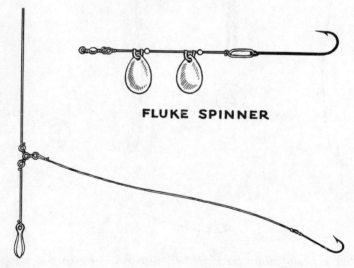

FLUKE SPINNER

This is a fluke rig showing a fluke spinner, which is often used instead of the plain hook.

called, a longer leader and larger hook are necessary. Carlisle hooks in sizes 4/0 to 6/0 are generally used, depending on the size of the fish. Here a leader from 2 to 3 ft. long is tied just above the sinker. Small, live killifish are often used as bait for fluke, and this arrangement allows them to move around a bit. Many anglers also add a double-bladed fluke spinner or a spoon-like flasher above the hook to attract the fish. Spinners work best in a fast tide or when the boat is drifting and the sinker is bouncing along the bottom.

When there are game fish such as weakfish, striped bass, bluefish and similar active feeders around, a "high-leader" rig is often effective. Here leaders as long as 5 or 6 ft. have been used, but 3- or 4-ft. leaders are easier to handle. If you are using the shorter version, it should be tied a distance equal to its length above a sinker which is heavy enough to reach bottom. The hook is then baited with a whole sandworm or bloodworm, a strip of squid, a chunk of shedder crab or a strip of fish and is lowered into the water. Care should be taken to see that the leader straightens out before you release the sinker. When the rig hits bottom, you lift the rod high, then lower it, at the same time letting out some line. When the sinker strikes bottom again, you let it lie there for a few seconds, then lift the rod tip again and lower it, releasing more line. In this way the rig moves out along the bottom with the tide or current, thus covering more territory and at the same time giving the bait some movement. When the rig has been taken out some distance from the boat you can reel in and repeat the process, or you can reel in very slowly, dragging the sinker along the bottom in the hope that a fish will see it.

The high-leader rig discussed above is sometimes used with another hook on a shorter leader or snell tied just above the sinker. Thus, while the more active and shallower

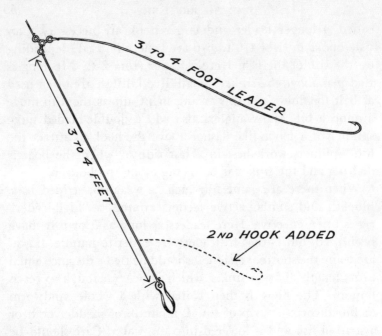

This is a diagram of the high-leader rig showing the optional second hook added near the sinker for bottom feeders.

feeding game fish can go for the upper hook the more sluggish bottom feeders can take the lower one.

Surf anglers who do bottom fishing with natural bait use two kinds of rigs. One is the standard surf rig, which is similar to the basic bottom rig except that the leaders are longer and a pyramid sinker is used instead of a bank sinker. The leader, which is usually from 18 to 24 in. long, is tied to a three-way swivel just above the sinker. Hooks will, of course, vary in size and pattern depending on the fish sought. Striped bass, bluefish, channel bass, weakfish, kingfish or whiting can all be taken in the surf with this rig.

The other rig used in surf fishing is the "fish-finder" rig.

It has a fish-finder gadget which has a round ring on one end and a snap on the other. The snap holds the sinker. The line is then run through the hole in the fish-finder and is tied to a leather thong which has been forced through one of the eyes of a large barrel swivel. If you have no leather thongs you can also tie the line directly to a big barrel swivel. Then the leader with the hook is tied to the other eye on the barrel swivel. The leather thong or barrel swivel acts as a stop to prevent the fish-finder and sinker from sliding down to the hook.

The theory behind this fish-finder rig is that when a fish picks up the bait it can move off with it without dragging the sinker. The line moves out freely through the ring on the fish-finder and while the angler can feel the pickup,

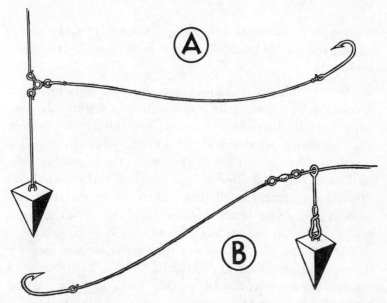

Two bottom rigs used in surf fishing. "A" is the standard surf rig on a three-way swivel. "B" is a surf rig with a "fish-finder."

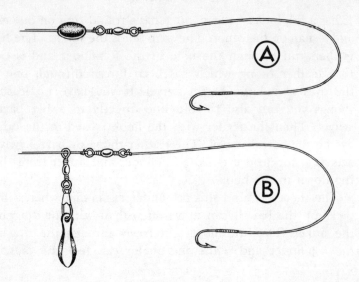

Two types of sliding-sinker rigs are shown. "A" makes use of an egg-shaped sinker. "B" uses a snap-swivel and a bank sinker.

the fish doesn't get suspicious and drop the bait for good. A cork can be added to the leader so that by letting out some slack line the bait can be carried well above the bottom and can move around and attract fish. Also with such a variation there is also less chance for crabs to eat the bait. In fact, it's a good idea to carry round corks with holes through the centers at all times when fishing the surf with natural bait. When crabs become troublesome, these corks can be added to the leaders of both rigs discussed above.

The rigs described above are the variety usually used for bottom fishing along the Atlantic Coast. There are, of course, some variations in certain areas and for certain kinds of fishing. It pays to watch closely how the veteran or successful angler makes up and uses his rig. Check such details as the size and pattern of the hooks being used; the length and thickness of the leaders or snells; the distance above the sinker they are tied; and the weight and style of the sinker that is needed. All of these play a part in presenting the bait to the fish properly.

Speaking of bait, the rig you use is worthless unless the bait you use is both correct and fresh. Try to find out in advance which bait the fish have been taking best, then buy or obtain enough bait to last until you quit fishing. If you don't know what bait is best on a given day or in a certain area it's wise to bring along three or four different kinds. Then you stand a better chance of having at least one bait which will catch fish. And nothing beats fresh bait. Buy the freshest you can obtain and change it on the hook often.

One final tip about rigs: I find it's a good idea to make up several rigs in advance before I go fishing. It takes time to make up a completed rig on a boat or on shore when you're actually fishing. With several on hand, you won't have to waste valuable minutes tying up a rig from scratch.

5

NATURAL BAITS AND HOW TO USE THEM

Although each year more and more salt-water anglers are using artificial lures, the great majority still depend on natural baits for their fishing. Indeed, many salt-water fish will not take artificial lures, except on rare occasions, and must be tempted with live bait. This is especially true with respect to bottom fishing, which is the most popular form of salt-water angling, where many so-called game fish will often ignore artificial lures and can be taken only on natural bait. Even fish which strike on artificial lures readily have certain periods and conditions when they prefer live bait.

It is true that fishing with artificial lures is sporting and a lot of fun and that it requires quite a bit of skill, but fishing with bait can also furnish fine sport and requires considerable knowledge, for you must know what baits to use, how to obtain them, how to keep them and how to hook them. The angler who knows his salt-water baits and how to use them generally catches more fish than the man who lacks this knowledge.

The bait fisherman should also remember that for best results his bait should be as lively and fresh as possible.

Another important thing to remember while bait fishing is to use the sharpest and strongest hooks possible. Hooks which are dull or which straighten out or snap off when a large fish takes hold account for the loss of many fish each season.

Salt-water bait fishing can be done with almost any type of rod and reel. For bottom fishing, the most popular rod is the one- or two-piece boat rod, but big-game, surf-casting, bait-casting, spinning and even fly-casting tackle can all be used with natural baits. The terminal rig used in bait fishing is important and this subject is covered in the previous chapter on using the right rig.

While most of the baits covered here can be bought from tackle stores, bait dealers or fish markets, many anglers pre-

A cast net like this is useful for catching mullet and other bait fish.

fer to obtain their own. The angler who gathers his own bait should check with his state and local laws. Many states and areas have laws governing the taking of such baits as sea worms, clams, crabs and bait fish.

Sea worms are a favorite bait with salt-water anglers since most fish take them and they are easy to obtain or buy and handy to keep and carry. The most popular sea worms are the "clamworms," also called "sandworms," along the Atlantic Coast and "mussel worms" along the Pacific Coast. Those commonly used belong to the genus *Nereis,* and there are several species on both coasts. One of those along the Pacific Coast reaches more than 3 ft. in length, but most clamworms average from 5 to 12 in. in length.

Clamworms are found in shelly sand and mud flats, among mussels and barnacles or piles and under stones. At night they leave their burrows and hiding places and can be picked up on tidal flats or scooped up in shallow water. At other times they can be obtained by digging deep with a clam hoe or fork on tidal flats at low tide.

Another popular sea worm is the bloodworm, also known as the "beak thrower," "four-jawed worm" and "proboscis worm." A number of species of bloodworms are found in the mud flats along both the Atlantic and Pacific coasts. They can be dug up with the same tools used for obtaining other sea worms. Like clamworms, they can be found near the low-water mark, but they usually lie deeper in the mud than clamworms.

Sea worms can be kept in damp rockweed in a cool cellar or icebox for several days. Occasionally, they should be sprinkled lightly with salt water, and any dead worms should be discarded each day.

Sea worms are used for striped bass, weakfish, croakers, flounders, porgies, tautog or blackfish and many other fish.

For large fish one, two or three whole worms on a hook are usually used. For trolling, one or more worms are hooked behind the spinner so as to leave the ends trailing through the water and fluttering attractively. A gang hook can be used to catch fish which strike short. And for small fish with tiny mouths, pieces of worm 1 or 2 in. in length are best.

There are many other kinds of sea worms, such as ribbon worms or tapeworms and lugworms, which can be used for bait. In fact, almost any sea worm of good size will be taken by salt-water fish. Even earthworms like night crawlers and garden worms are used at times to catch salt-water fish such as flounders.

Another popular bait with salt-water anglers are clams. These bivalve mollusks are numerous along both the Atlantic and Pacific Coasts, where they live in the mud and sand of beaches, inlets, bays and the ocean. There are many species and almost all of them make good bait. One of the most widely used on the Atlantic Coast is the big surf clam, also known as the sea clam and skimmer clam. Another common and popular clam is the ordinary hardshell clam found in restaurants and fish markets and often referred to as quahog, round clam and littleneck. Still another clam is the softshell, also known as the long-necked clam, steamer clam and sand clam. It is found in sandy mud flats along the Atlantic and parts of the Pacific. There are also many other clams, such as the pismo clam, gaper clam, geoduck clam and the razor or jackknife clam, which can be used for bait when available.

Most clams can be bought from bait dealers and fish markets or they can be obtained along beaches or in bays, where they bury themselves in the sand or mud. You can wade in shallow water, look for them or feel them with your bare feet and then dig them out. On exposed flats at low tide you can also dig many clams with a clam hoe or fork.

Clams will stay alive for several days if kept in a cool spot or on ice. For longer periods, they should be submerged in salt water in a box. Clams, of course, must be shucked or removed from their hard shells. This can be done by inserting a knife blade between the two shells and cutting the muscles which hold them together. But to save time, work, and a possible injury to the hands most anglers crack the shells by just hitting them against a hard object.

For big fish such as striped bass and cod the insides of one or more large clams are draped on a hook. The siphon or neck of most clams makes a good tough bait if the dark skin is removed to reveal the light meat. For small fish such as blackfish or tautog, porgies, flounders and others with small mouths, tiny pieces of clam are best.

Mussels, which are found in the ocean, bays and other salt waters, can also be used as bait. They can easily be gathered from jetties, pilings and rocks at low tide. Mussels are a soft bait and do not stay on the hook too well, but they can be tied down with thread. Some anglers steam, boil or dry out mussels a bit to toughen them. They are also used as chum to attract salt-water fish and can either be crushed and thrown overboard a little at a time or placed in a chum pot or wire cage and lowered into the water.

Then there are many other mollusks, such as conchs, sea snails, abalone, whelks and periwinkles, which are used as bait. In fact, almost any salt-water shellfish, if large enough to make a practical bait, can be used.

Crabs are eaten by many salt-water fish and make good bait in any of the various stages that they occur. Crabs shed their hard covering at regular intervals as they grow, and most fish prefer to eat them when they are in the soft, helpless stage. Just before they shed their hard covering, they are known as shedder or peeler crabs. After they shed their shells they are known as soft-shell crabs, and when their new shell starts to harden but still caves in when pressed, they are called paper-backs or leather-backs. Finally the shell hardens completely and they become hard crabs again. While crabs can be used as bait in all their stages, those which are in the soft-shell or shedder stages are best.

Among the crabs popular for bait are the blue crab which is the one found in restaurants and fish markets along the Atlantic 'and Gulf coasts. Other crabs used for bait are lady crabs, also called calico crabs, fiddler crabs, hermit crabs and green crabs.

Crabs can be bought in fish markets and from bait dealers. They can also be caught by hand with long-handled nets, on lines baited with meat or fish and in various types of traps. For short periods of time, crabs may be kept in damp seaweed on ice, while for longer periods they should be put in wire cages and submerged in salt water.

Crabs will catch striped bass, channel bass, weakfish, blackfish or tautog, sheepshead, bonefish and many other salt-water fish. Whole large crabs are best for big fish. Small whole crabs or sections of large crabs are best for smaller fish. Hard crabs can be hooked through the body, between the legs or in the hole left when the large claws are removed. Hermit crabs can be removed from their shell homes and threaded on the hook with the point and barb reaching into the soft tail-section. Soft-shell crabs and shedder crabs are often lashed on the hook with fine thread.

If you can resist eating them, the common lobster and the spiny lobster can be used for bait. The tail sections are used after the hard covering has been removed. Shrimps and prawns are numerous in species and numbers in practically all salt waters. All shrimp make good bait, from edible or jumbo shrimps to tiny sand shrimps, grass shrimps or common prawns. They can often be purchased at fish markets or

A tandem hook such as this can be used to hook dead bait fish.

bait dealers. Or you can search for the smaller varieties in bays and tidal creeks among the eelgrass, where they can be caught in fine-meshed dip nets or seines.

Shrimp can be kept in a wire cage submerged in the water or in damp sawdust or seaweed on ice. Large shrimps are usually removed from their shells and the meat from the tail threaded on the hook. Smaller shrimps are used whole and are hooked through the body or tail segments. Shrimp will take striped bass, weakfish, flounders, tautog or blackfish, bonefish, snappers and many other salt-water fish. Small shrimps are also good as chum when thrown overboard a few at a time and will attract fish such as weakfish and striped bass. Sand bugs or sand fleas, which are found in the sand where ocean waves break on the beaches, can be dug out of the stand or caught in special traps and used for striped bass, blackfish and pompano.

But of all the baits used for salt-water game fish, bait fish as a group are no doubt the most productive. These small fish usually average from 3 to 12 in. in length and include many species. Silvery mullets are near the top of the list with respect to both popularity and productivity. Two species—the striped mullet and the white mullet—are most commonly used. Menhaden or mossbunker is also highly favored because of its abundance and oily flesh, which attracts most salt-water fish. It is especially popular as chum when ground or chopped up and used to attract bluefish, tuna and mackerel.

Other members of the varied and prolific herring family, such as the common herring, Pacific herring, sardines, pilchards and alewives, are widely used. Anchovies make good bait, especially in the Pacific Ocean, where they are used as chum and bait for barracuda, yellowtail, albacore and halibut. Minnows of the sea along the Atlantic and Gulf coasts include the many species of spearing or silversides. They travel in large schools and are effective for striped bass, weakfish, bluefish, summer flounder or fluke, silver hake and other fish. The hardy killifish or mummichog, found in bays and inlets, lives a long time on the hook. It is favored for summer flounder, small bluefish and sea bass. Sand eels or launces are also numerous and popular baits. The common eel is occasionally used alive or cut up into chunks for bottom fishing. But it is more commonly used for striped

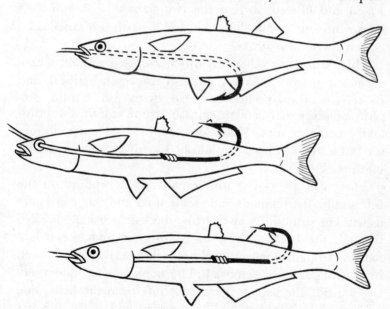

Dead bait fish can be hooked by the methods shown here.

bass, rigged whole with two hooks so as to give it a motion like an artificial lure. Eelskins, when attached to eelskin lures, are also used for striped bass, bluefish, weakfish and other fish.

Bait fish can be bought in fish markets and tackle stores, and from bait dealers and commercial fishermen. They can also be caught with seines, cast nets, funnel-type traps and drop or umbrella nets. Most bait fish are rather delicate and to keep them alive for any length of time you must put them in live boxes submerged in water. But some of them, like the common eels and the killifish, are quite hardy and can be kept alive for hours in damp seaweed placed in a cool spot.

The methods commonly used in baiting the bait fish are shown in the illustration on page 69. Large bait fish should be scaled and filleted, so that the two slabs of flesh can then be cut into any size or shape desired. Big bait fish can also be cut crosswise into steaks.

There are many other fish which are used as bait. These include common mackerel, Spanish mackerel, halfbeak and its relative, the ballyhoo or balao, flying fish, bonito, dolphin, albacore, barracuda, bonefish, grunt, catfish, butterfish and whiting or silver hake. Most of these are used offshore for salt-water fish such as sailfish, swordfish, the tunas and marlins.

These fish are rigged in various ways depending on the fish sought, the methods and tackle used and the area being fished. For still-fishing or drifting, the bait is usually hooked through the back or lips. In trolling, to give the bait a natural wriggling movement the backbone is either broken in several places or removed. The hook can be hidden entirely inside the bait or it can protrude from the belly, side or back. The hooks should be sewn in and if the fish has been slit open the belly cavity should also be sewn up. The

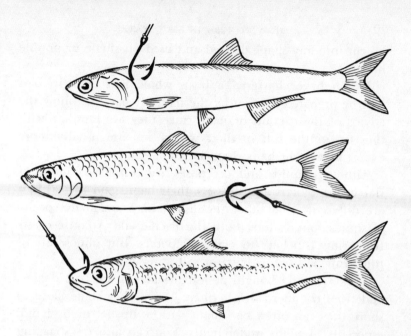

Live, delicate bait fish such as herring, anchovies and sardines can be hooked as shown above.

mouth and gills can be sewn up to keep the water out and prevent the bait from revolving when trolled.

Many of these same fish are also used for strip bait, which are trolled through the water in offshore fishing. Here the shiny sides or white belly of the fish are cut into long, narrow, thin strips anywhere from 8 to 14 in. in length—wide in the middle and tapering to points at each end. The edges of strip bait are usually thinned down. Next a wire leader is attached to the hook, forming a safety-pin catch. Then the strip is slit in two spots, one near the center of the bait and the other near the head. The hook is run through the slit near the center of the bait and the safety-pin catch is fastened to the other hole. Strip bait can also be cut into any shape desired and used on single or double hooks.

If you have chartered a boat, whole bait or strip bait will be prepared for you by the mate. It pays to follow the advice of the captain or mate since they are familiar with the way of the fish in their waters and are usually more expert at rigging baits than most anglers.

Although squids and octopuses are considered mollusks like clams, oysters and mussels, their habits and uses as bait are different from other shellfish. There are many species of squids found along both the Pacific and Atlantic coasts from tiny 1-inchers to giant 50-footers. But almost all of them can be used as bait for salt-water fish.

Squids can be bought at fish markets, from bait dealers and from commercial fishermen. When they come close to shore they can often be caught with a dip net or by hand, especially at night under lights. You can also try snagging them with a treble hook baited with a small bait fish.

Squids are difficult to keep alive, but they can be frozen whole or cleaned and cut into strips and salted down in jars. Fresh squids are used whole for swordfish, marlin and striped bass, while the head, tentacles or strips from the body can be used for striped bass, bluefish, weakfish, channel bass, cod, summer flounder and other salt-water fish.

The squid's cousin, the octopus, also can be used to catch salt-water fish in the waters where it is found. They can be caught in shallow pools at low tide with gaff hooks or spears. You can also turn over rocks and look for them among coral reefs in tropical waters. It makes a tough bait and the tentacles can be cut to any size.

Finally, almost anything that crawls or swims and is large enough to make a practical bait can be tried for salt-water fish. It pays to experiment and try several kinds of bait when you go fishing. The angler who brings along a variety of baits stands less chance of being skunked. In the vast ocean with its innumerable varieties of fish that come and go with the tides, you never know what kind of fish to expect and what kind of food or bait is present. By carrying several kinds of bait you are better prepared to meet these changing conditions.

6

TIDES—THE KEY TO GOOD FISHING

We had been fishing from a boat for porgies, and these pan fish of the sea were providing fast action. The minute the sinker hit bottom, the clam bait would be grabbed and a quick lift of the rod tip would set the hook. Then the porgies would be reeled to the top—we had many "double-headers," two porgies at the same time on one line. Most of the boats around us were also catching them. Then suddenly, as if on a given signal, they stopped biting and our baited hooks stayed in the water without so much as a nibble. I noticed that the other boats in the area weren't doing anything either.

"What happened? Looks like they've either stopped biting or gone away," one of the anglers on our boat remarked.

I glanced at my watch and then said, "We might as well have something to eat. There won't be anything doing for at least an hour."

"How come? How do you know when they'll start biting again?" my friend asked.

"It's slack water. Porgies usually bite best when the tide is running," I explained.

So we sat down and had a leisurely lunch while waiting for

the tide to change and start coming in again. About an hour later we resumed fishing and the porgies started biting with their former zest and rapidity.

Another time I was fishing for striped bass with an expert surf angler up in Rhode Island. The ocean was like glass—flat, calm and with no sign of fish. The sun was rising higher and it didn't look too good. In fact, I was beginning to have my doubts about catching any striped bass that day.

"It doesn't look like there will be anything doing today," I commented.

"Don't you worry. Just wait another half-hour or so. They'll show!" my expert friend stated with authority. Sure enough, about a half-hour later the whole ocean seemed to erupt with feeding stripers and we enjoyed some fast fishing.

"How did you know when they would show up?" I asked the old-time surf angler. "It was easy. I was here yesterday morning when they showed under the same water conditions. So I merely added one hour more to yesterday's appearance to account for the later tide today!"

It sounds like black magic but a thorough knowledge of tides and their influence on fishing in your area pays big dividends. It's one key to success in salt-water fishing. Charter-boat captains and fishing guides know this and make a close study of tides, currents and their effects on the fishing in their areas.

Many casual salt-water anglers, on the other hand, pay little attention to the tides and currents and then wonder why they don't catch as many fish as the other guy does. Still other anglers realize that tides have some effect upon their fishing, but they do not know why this is so or exactly how tides influence the fishing. Such anglers often waste precious hours casting, trolling or sinker bouncing when the tide is wrong. But the salt-water angler who knows tides can pick the favorable fishing periods in advance and concentrate his efforts during such times. It means fewer wasted days and more fish on the beach or in the boat.

We won't go into the science of tides here except to mention that tides are caused by the gravitational forces of both the moon and the sun. The moon, being nearer the earth than the sun has the greater influence on the earth's waters. When the tide rises the water moves toward land and it is then known as the flood tide. When it drops and

Tides play a big part in surf fishing. At low tide surf anglers usually go out to the end of a jetty for the best fishing.

moves back to sea it is called the ebb tide. The "slack" tide is the period when the tide moves neither way. It takes about 6 hours for the tide to go from low to high and 6 hours from high to low. Every 24 hours the tides occur approximately 50 minutes later.

Tides also vary in the degrees to which they rise or drop. When the moon and sun are on the same side of the earth in a direct line the combined influence causes the highest tides. These are known as the spring tides and occur during the full-moon and new-moon periods. At this time the tides are both higher and lower than usual in a given area. During the first quarter and last quarter phases of the moon the tides do not rise or fall as much. These are known as the neap tides.

Tides are important to all salt-water fishermen, but no group studies them as intensely as the surf anglers. These hard-working men with the long sticks know that tides are vital in surf fishing. Most veteran surf anglers "fish the tides": They go out when they believe a certain stage of the tide is most favorable for the area being fished. Usually they have acquired this information the hard way: through "trial-and-error" fishing of a certain area for many years. They get so they can often predict in advance which tides are best for a given location.

Naturally the novice surf angler fishing a new area doesn't have this information and can't put it to use. However, there are helpful tips and general rules about tides which can be applied to surf fishing. For example, as in boat fishing, a moving tide or current is usually more productive than no tide or current. So you'll find that "slack" water rarely provides good fishing in the surf.

The start of the incoming tide is one of the most productive periods for surf fishing, especially for such gamesters as striped bass, bluefish, weakfish and channel bass. During slack water smaller bait fish often tend to scatter, and with no strong currents they can swim fast and escape the larger fish. But when the tide starts to move, these small bait fish are at the mercy of the strong currents and rips. Then the stripers and other game fish find them easier to catch. The start of the outgoing tide is also good for the same reason. In fact, the so-called change of tide, whether it occurs at low water or high water, is the time to be down at the beach casting.

When using artificial lures in the surf, I personally prefer low tides to high tides. At least that is when I have made my best catches, especially of striped bass. My belief is that at this point the bait fish are more concentrated in small areas such as holes, channels, sloughs and similar deep-water spots. Larger game fish also tend to gather to feed on these concentrations of bait fish. So at low tide they are actively feeding and easier to locate. Also the low tides produce more white water on the sand bars, mussel bars, rocky reefs and boulders. The crashing of the waves over these shallow-water spots creates a surf and makes it easier to fool fish such as stripers, channel bass and others.

However, when the tide drops and gets too low, there may not be enough water on the sand bars, rocky reefs and mussel beds to float a good-sized fish. At such times, it is often possible to wade out on the bars and fish the outer edge where there is deeper water.

When fishing near an inlet emptying into the surf, I've had my best fishing in the last of the outgoing tide and start of the incoming. The water moving out often sweeps schools of bait fish along and the incoming waves crashing against this current creates a turmoil which makes easy pickings for larger game fish.

When surf fishing where there are rock jetties, you will also have good results when the tide is low. Most jetties of this kind are broken up, and at high tide they are covered with water and too dangerous to fish because of the waves. So at high tide I usually fish from the beach itself or on the back of the jetty. But after the tide has dropped I move out on the jetty and work toward the front when it is safe. Near low water, the end of the jetty is usually best since you can cast out into deeper water.

Along rocky shores such as those found in Rhode Island, parts of Massachusetts and at Montauk, New York, the formation of the shoreline governs which tide is most productive. Here, for example, you'll often find coves and rocky reefs which are exposed or barely covered at low tide. Such spots are usually best when the tide is near its high point. If there are scattered boulders which are partly exposed, the best tides here are usually those which produce white water when the waves crash over these rocks. Striped bass like to lie on the shore side of such boulders. Then there are rocky points and rock or mussel bars which run out into deeper water a good distance. These are usually best when the tide is near its low point and you can wade out on them.

Surf anglers who know certain areas and how they are affected by the different stages of the tide can often fish two or three spots during one tide. For example, I remember fishing in Rhode Island one fall and catching five stripers near the Pt. Judith lighthouse. It was high tide and this spot produces well under these conditions especially when there is rough surf. Then, after the tide dropped, I drove down to Charlestown Beach a few miles to the west and caught ten more striped bass. Here there's an inlet, and the best fishing usually takes place between half tide and low water.

Surf anglers aren't the only ones who can take advantage

of the different stages of the tide. Bridge fishermen, too, can work the trick of hitting the best spots at the right time and tide. Some bridge fishermen in the Miami, Florida, area are past masters at this game. This is especially true of those who seek gamesters such as ladyfish and snook. Ladyfish like to feed under bridges at the start of the outgoing tide. Since this stage of the tide may be early at one bridge and later at another, the anglers fish one bridge, then jump into their cars and head for the next one where the tide is a bit later. A real expert at this game can often work several bridges in one night and get action at each one.

Much the same thing can be done by the angler fishing tidal creeks for such fish as striped bass and weakfish. On the incoming tide the smart angler can move and change his location from one spot to another, following the tide as it increases in strength and creates eddies and rips at different places. Then, on the outgoing tide, he can work his way back over the same river or tidal creek. Points of land or rocks, sandbars, partly sunken boulders, islands, piers, rock and bridge pilings can be fished on one end or side during the incoming tide and on the opposite end or side on the outgoing tide.

In southern waters such as those in Florida—especially the area around the Everglades and the Ten Thousand Islands —the tides play a big part in the fishing. If you are seeking snook or tarpon in this maze of mangroves, winding creeks and channels, you'd better know your tides. They run in all directions and the channels are so complicated that the tide may vary in different places by three hours or more. If you come too early you may not find enough water for fishing or even to float your boat. If you wait too long in some places you can find yourself stranded and may have to wait for high tide again. As a general rule the best fishing in the Ever-

Anglers who fish for bonefish in the Florida Keys pay close attention to the tides and usually begin fishing at the start of the incoming tide.

glades takes place around high water, when the mangrove roots are covered. Then snook like to lie among the roots under the trees. At the lower tides they drop back to channels and holes, where they can often be caught.

Or take bonefishing. Every bonefisherman knows that the best time to go after these fish is when the tide starts to come in and cover the flats. Then the white ghosts move in singly, in pairs or small schools, seeking the crabs, worms and shellfish found on the flats. They move against the tide, as most fish do when actively feeding. The outgoing tide is often good for bonefish, but when the tide is near low your best chances of catching bonefish is in the deeper water along the edges of flats or channels.

Even when you are fishing offshore in salt water, your chances may be affected by the tides. When you are chumming at anchor for tuna, albacore, bonito, bluefish and similar fish there should be a tide running. If the tide is slack, the chum sinks straight down under the boat and rarely attracts the game fish. But a running tide carries the chum away from the boat. The tide also forms a slick and carries tidbits to fish which may be in the area, as well as giving the bait some movement and catching the attention of the fish. On the other hand, too strong a tide will often kill the fishing by floating the chum too fast and too far away from the boat and causing the baited hook to ride too near the surface.

Finally, a salt-water angler familiar with tides and how they affect the area he is fishing can often predict good fishing periods well in advance. By consulting the tide and current tables ahead of time he can tell when a certain spot will have the stage of tide which produces best for that area. Thus he can pinpoint, days, weeks and even months in advance, the time and place he will do his fishing. Although many newspapers and some magazines print tide tables, the best source for this information is the *Tide Tables* and *Current Tables,* prepared and issued by the U. S. Coast and Geodetic Survey. These two books can be bought in many marine supply houses or they can be obtained from the U. S. Government Printing Office in Washington, D. C.

It's surprising how many salt-water anglers go fishing without even knowing when high tide or low tide occurs. They act as if tides make little or no difference in salt-water fishing. Such anglers waste many hours fishing at the wrong time when they could concentrate their efforts on the best tidal periods and catch more fish in less time.

7

THE DEADLY ART OF CHUMMING

The basic idea behind chumming is to encourage fish to eat something with no hooks attached in the hope that they will later take something with a hook. Chumming also attracts fish in large numbers to a certain spot. Instead of the angler moving about in search of fish, he can stay in one spot and wait for the fish to come to him. Mainly, however, the idea is to fool the fish with a free handout and dispel his suspicions so that he will more readily take a baited hook.

Various methods and techniques are used in chumming, and the angler who knows and practices them will often catch fish when ordinary casting or trolling methods fail to produce. You'll find a long list of game fish and bottom fish which respond to chumming like a gang of hungry ranch hands to a dinner bell. In fact, to catch certain fish chumming is almost a must.

Take the giant tuna, for example. Although a few big fish are caught by trolling or drifting with whole fish baits, the great majority of tuna fishermen depend on chumming to get results. They use ground menhaden or mossbunker, called "bunker" for short. This flat, deep bodied fish, which averages about a foot in length, is seined commercially for its oil. Millions of pounds are caught annually. And each year more and more of these fish are being diverted for use in chumming. In three days, the U. S. Atlantic Tuna Tournament has been known to use up 85,000 lbs. of bunker chum.

Menhaden or bunker can now be bought fresh, iced or frozen, either by the bushel or in cans or blocks. Whole bunker are sold by the bushel and must be ground by the angler. Those sold in cans or frozen in blocks are already ground and ready to use. The usual method of chumming begins with the acquisition of a big container, such as a garbage can, filled with sea water. The ground mossbunker is then added and the whole mess is stirred around until it is the consistency of a thick soup. Then one or two anglers start ladling the stuff over the side of the boat in order to form a chum slick. In this slick, the oil spreads in a broad band on the surface of the water and extends for several hundred feet behind the boat. The particles of bunker sink to varying depths under the chum slick. Tuna and other fish get the scent of the oil and juices and follow it up to the boat.

Most tuna fishermen also get whole bunker and cut them into big chunks, which they toss overboard into the chum slick as an added attraction. Butterfish, mackerel, herring and whiting can also be cut up and thrown out. This gives the tuna something to swallow and holds their interest.

Next, of course, you bait up a big tuna hook with a whole bunker, herring, mackerel, butterfish or whiting and let it drift out naturally in the chum line. Finally you hope a big tuna will take it.

Another method of chumming for tuna is practiced at Wedgeport, Nova Scotia. Here, instead of ground chum, they use whole herring. These are tossed out into the water in the tide behind the boat. The fishermen also make up

Anglers seeking giant tuna usually chum with herring or bunkers. This one was caught at Wedgeport, Nova Scotia.

a "teaser" or "grapevine" consisting of a dozen or so herring tied about a foot apart on a cord. These are trailed behind the boat, where the tuna are attracted by the splash and ripples the herring make on the surface. To the fish it looks like a school of bait fish, and they will often come up and grab a herring from the teaser. In the meantime, the angler lets out a hook with another herring on it and hopes a tuna will come up and swallow it.

Whole bait fish are also used on the "live-bait" boats which leave from many ports in Southern California. These boats are equipped with big bait tanks, where sardines and anchovies can be kept alive. The live bait fish are thrown into the water a few at a time. This brings around such game fish as tuna, yellowtail, albacore, bonito and barracuda. When a fish is hooked or seen swirling behind the boat, the anglers put a live anchovy or sardine on a hook, cast it out and let it swim around in the water. In this type of fishing, it is important to use small hooks and fine leaders in order to fool the fish.

When it comes to catching bluefish, chumming is by far the most effective and productive method. Here, too, ground menhaden or bunker is used, and from June to October tons of chum are dumped into the water along the Atlantic Coast to attract blues. This chumming is mostly done off the coasts of New York and New Jersey. On a weekend you'll often see a fleet of several hundred boats all chumming for bluefish. And the fishing is not only done during the daytime but continues into the night. During the day the boats usually drift with the tide and wind while dispensing the chum. At night they usually anchor. However, if the tide or wind is too strong, anchoring is the best procedure, day or night.

When chumming for bluefish a chunk of butterfish or bunker is generally used on a hook and this is let out in the chum slick with the tide. In the beginning you may have to let out up to 150 ft. of line to get a strike from a bluefish. But as the fish work into the chum slick they come closer and closer to the boat. If they are really feeding in the chum they will often come close to the top. Then you will get

Chumming is widely practiced in catching bluefish like these, but it is also effective for many other salt-water species.

your strikes soon after the bait is dropped into the water. However, when the tide is strong or when the fish are deep you may have to add a clincher sinker on the leader to get the bait down to where the fish are feeding. Also, if you have to get the bait down deep, let out plenty of slack line from the reel.

If a bluefish takes the bait, the line will run off the reel rapidly. That's why the reel should be set in free-spool and held lightly with the thumb. When a fish picks up the bait, let him run for a few seconds, then throw the drag on and set the hook.

During August and September along the Atlantic Coast, when you are chumming for bluefish, you'll often notice false albacore and bonito feeding on the chum. They will often take a hook baited with a piece of bunker or butterfish, but they are more shy of hooks and leaders than blues and consequently harder to hook. When they show up in the chum we usually put the heavier bluefish rod aside, take out a light salt-water spinning outfit and go after them with that. We attach a small white or yellow bucktail jig to the end of the 8-lb. test line. Then we cast out into the chum slick and as the jig sinks we jerk it sharply and then let it drop back again. We continue doing this until we get a strike.

I remember one day when both bluefish and bonito showed up in the chum slick and started feeding on top. We used small surface popping plugs, and after the cast we worked them through the chum slick toward the boat. Talk about action! On almost every cast the bluefish or bonito would swirl behind the plug, and every so often one would take it. This is real sport on a light spin outfit, and it was chumming that made it possible to bring the fish up to the boat and get them into a feeding mood.

Another popular game fish which is often caught by chumming is the northern weakfish or squeteague. The chum usually used here is small grass shrimp. These tiny, translucent shrimp can be bought by the quart from bait dealers and boat liveries in the popular weakfish areas in New Jersey, New York and New England. However, using them is expensive since you'll need anywhere from 4 to 8 qts. for a day's fishing. So many weakfishermen try to catch their own shrimp in tidal bays and creeks. A seine with a fine mesh can be used for this.

Chumming for weakfish with grass shrimp is also done from an anchored boat in a channel or deep hole. It is most effective when there's a moderate tide or current running. At first you throw out a few shrimp at a time to start things going. Then, when the fish appear in the chum streak, you can cut it down to two or three shrimp at a throw, but you must work steadily without prolonged breaks. In this type of fishing you use a light spinning rod or a bait-casting rod and rig a small No. 1 or 2 hook on a long nylon leader. Then you bait it with a whole sandworm or two or more small grass shrimp, after which you pull line off the reel and let the baited hook drift naturally in the chum streak. After letting the line out about 150 ft. you reel it in again and then lit it drift out again. The weakfish will usually come to the top and take the hook.

However, when the fish are in very deep water or when the tide is slack, fishing near the bottom is often more effective. Here you fish with a sinker and a hook on a long leader tied about 3 or 4 ft. above the sinker. On slack water you can try chumming with grass shrimp, but first squeeze or pinch the shrimp so that they will sink instead of swim away. Besides shrimp, you can also use squid for chum when weakfishing. You'll need several pounds and it must be diced into small pieces. Strips of the squid make a good bait for weakfish when you are fishing on the bottom.

The same grass shrimp can also be used to attract the smaller striped bass found in inlets, bays and creeks. This method is used in Chesapeake Bay, but it will also work in most bay waters where stripers are found.

Chumming for the larger striped bass found in the surf was widely practiced at one time. The early striped-bass fishing clubs and private bass stands at Martha's Vineyard and Cuttyhunk in Massachusetts and along the Rhode Island coast were scenes for this type of fishing. Here they used to hire a man who would chum for several hours or even all night before the fishermen arrived. The chummer used menhaden, which was also used for bait. They also used lobster tails for striped-bass bait, but then lobsters were cheap in those days, small ones selling for $1.50 per hundred.

Today chumming for striped bass in the surf is only done on rare occasions. It is hard work and the menhaden aren't as cheap as they used to be. Also, with more surf anglers than ever fishing, chummers have little privacy. It can be discouraging to chum all night or all day and then have other anglers fish a couple of hundred feet below you and catch striped bass which you attracted to the area. But that's a risk you take today no matter what kind of chumming you do. The waters are so crowded that it is a common thing to see your chum slick spoiled by boats cutting across it. Other wiseacres will anchor just below your boat and fish in your chum slick.

Chumming is a sure-fire method when fishing for sharks. These fish depend a great deal on their sense of smell to locate their food. So they'll soon come around if you start chumming. Here, too, the usual chum is ground menhaden, which is dispensed freely while drifting at night. Every so often a small fish or two can be tossed overboard to drift down the chum streak. If you can get a couple of buckets of beef blood you can also use this as chum. In fact, the blood of almost any fish or animal will attract sharks. You can also cut open a fish or two and suspend them alongside of the boat. The bloodier kinds of fish, such as tuna, albacore and bonito, are best for this. Chunks of these fish or small ones also make good bait for sharks.

In recent years fishermen have also discovered that mackerel, especially the common Atlantic variety, can be brought up to a boat with menhaden chum. Then they will take artificial lures, such as small spoons, metal squids and diamond jigs, under the boat.

Both summer flounder or fluke and winter flounder are attracted by chum. The angler who chums for these fish usually makes better catches than those who don't. I remember on several occasions chumming for bluefish with ground bunker when I'd hook fluke, which would take the bunker or butterfish bait on the hook if it sank deep enough. At such times you can change to a bottom rig and catch more fluke if you want to.

When fishing for smaller winter flounder, it's a good idea to bring along a bushel of mussels. You can crack the shell on these or mash them up and scatter them around the anchored boat. Another gimmick is to fill a mesh bag with cracked mussels and lower it over the side to the bottom. Some anglers make or buy special chum pots which are small wire cages and fill them with cracked mussels. Clams, oysters and scallops can also be used with or instead of the mussels. You may have to put a rock or some other weight into the bag or chum pot to sink it to the bottom in a fast current. Every so often you should bounce the bag or chum pot on the bottom to release the juices and fragments of meat in the surrounding water.

Many other bottom fishes, such as codfish, porgies, sea bass, sheepshead, blackfish or tautog, snappers and groupers can be chummed. In fact, the most successful codfishermen and blackfishermen in certain areas bait a spot for a day or two before fishing. They scatter cracked clams and mussels to bring the fish around.

In clear tropical waters such as those around Florida, Bermuda and the Bahamas, you can see the fish respond to your chum. Larger fish such as mullet or needlefish can be cut up into small pieces and thrown overboard. Smaller bait fish can be used whole, dead or alive, as chum. Spiny lobsters, shrimp heads, crushed crabs and diced conch can also be used. As these are scattered in the water you'll see fish of all kinds rising from the coral reefs for the tidbits. Then a hook baited with small bait fish, shrimp or pieces of mullet can be lowered to the waiting fish.

Chumming isn't a lazy man's game, and it is best done with two or three anglers taking turns so that one man can rest and get a chance to fish. But as far as results are concerned it is well worth the trouble. On certain days it may mean the difference between catching fish or going home with no fish. So to be assured of sport and fun the next time you go fishing try the deadly art of chumming.

8

HOW TO DRIFT-FISH

We had spent most of the morning cruising around in my friend's 22-ft. boat, searching for bluefish. We were off Rockaway Point, New York, where schools of small bluefish had been seen a couple of days earlier. My friend, Jack, suddenly pointed inshore and yelled, "Look—birds working!" I peered toward the spot and saw a big flock of gulls wheeling and diving about a half a mile away. Jack pulled on the gas throttle and the boat shot forward at full speed.

As we neared the area I could see terns diving into the flat, glassy water, and every so often I could see a swirl or splash that indicated a feeding fish. I rigged up a couple of rods after trolling, with a spoon on one and a rubber-tube lure on the other. I let the two lines out behind the boat, and we slowed down to trolling speed as we neared the edge of the feeding school of fish.

I could now see that there was a big school of fish because the swirls and breaks covered an area of several acres. When the boat reached the first few feeding fish we started to troll along the edge of the school. A minute later one of the rods dipped and the click on the reel started to screech. I grabbed the rod and could feel a fish fighting on the end. Then the other rod bent into an arc and I yelled to Jack, "Grab the other rod! There's another fish on!" Jack stopped the boat and took the other rod out of the holder. We had a hectic time keeping the two lines from fouling but managed to land two bluefish, each about 3 or 4 lbs.

By this time we were surrounded by other boats trolling through the school, and most of the fish had disappeared. The commotion had driven them into deeper water. Then we saw birds working again a few hundred feet away. We raced toward the scene and started to troll again. We picked up another bluefish before the other boats arrived and scared the fish away again.

Now I took out my light salt-water spinning outfit and attached a surface popping plug to the end of the leader. Jack rigged up a similar outfit and we started searching for the bluefish again. We saw the birds working in the distance and sped toward the spot as fast as possible.

"Let's try drifting this time. Run the boat up to the edge of the school of fish and cut the motor," I suggested to Jack. He did exactly as recommended, and when the boat stopped and started to drift slowly with the tide we could see bluefish breaking all around us; some of them only about 20 ft. from the boat.

I cast out the small popping plug and started to work it back toward the boat. I reeled and jerked it so that it threw a big splash. Almost immediately there was a swirl behind it, but the fish missed the lure. However, a second later it came back, grabbed it, splashed around the surface and then ran all over the place. On the light salt-water spinning rod it put up a much better scrap than it would have on the heavier trolling rod. Finally, I got it close to the boat and Jack netted it. It was another bluefish—about 3 lbs. in weight.

Then Jack hooked a fish on his light rod as the boat drifted through the feeding fish. Unlike the notice they would have taken of a trolling boat, the feeding fish paid little attention to the slowly drifting boat, and we had a half hour of fast action before the fish went down. We soon found another school and repeated the procedure over and over until we had caught a dozen blues and one bonito.

Similarly, on many other occasions I have found that when a trolling boat scares fish away, it is wise to resort to drifting. This is especially true when fish are feeding on the surface in clear, flat, calm water. At such times a trolling boat will often put them down. But a boat drifting quietly through the school rarely frightens the feeding fish.

The art of drift-fishing is not as well-known as trolling or fishing from an anchored boat. Of course, party boats which seek certain bottom fish often drift for these fish. Among these are the boats seeking fluke or summer flounder on the East Coast and the California halibut party boats on the West Coast. The so-called "drift" party boats in Florida waters also do a lot of drift-fishing for groupers, snappers, grunts and similar fish.

However, anglers fishing from private craft or rented skiffs tend to overlook drift-fishing. They know that fluke or summer flounder are usually caught by drifting, but they rarely try this method on other fish. Yet it has been my experience that almost every kind of bottom fish that swims can be taken by drift-fishing.

Drift-fishing offers several advantages over fishing at anchor. First, of course, you cover more territory. As the boat moves along, the baited hook follows and is seen by more fish than if it is left in one place. Second, a moving bait attracts more fish than one which lies on the bottom, where it often gets buried in seaweed and sand or falls into a crevice. Third, a moving bait seems to attract larger fish than a stationary one. Small bottom fish tend to congregate in compact schools around stationary bait and either steal it or get

Party boats drift for many fish while the anglers line up on one side of the boat.

caught. But a moving bait is often overtaken only by the larger members of most species. It also attracts more so-called true game fish than a stationary one. Last, but not least, drift-fishing eliminates the necessity of dropping an anchor and then hauling it up again.

The fact that your bait is always moving into a new area while drift-fishing also works in your favor in another way. When you anchor you may attract a few fish to your bait, but after you catch a few fish and miss others, the remaining ones often become suspicious. Then it's difficult to make them bite. But when you are drifting you are continually showing your bait to *new* fish which haven't been alerted.

Drift-fishing is most productive for bottom fish when there

are large areas such as banks, sand or rock bars, reefs, mussel beds, oyster beds, and etc., where fish are dispersed over a wide area. This is often the case when you seek such species as fluke or summer flounder, halibut, cod, haddock, sea bass, porgies, snappers, groupers, grunts and croakers which often tend to disperse themselves over a broad area.

Drift-fishing is less productive with species which tend to congregate around sunken wrecks, rock piles, holes or other obstructions which do not cover a wide area. However, you can often locate such spots while drifting and then anchor there to fish.

Best results are obtained in drift-fishing when there is a light or moderate wind or tide. The boat should move steadily—not too slow or too fast. If there is no wind and the tide is weak, the boat stays almost in one place. If there is a strong wind or tide, the boat moves too fast and it's difficult to keep your sinker and bait on the bottom. I remember on one occasion while I was drifting for fluke off New Jersey the wind was about 25 m.p.h. We moved so fast that the sinker was off the bottom most of the time. We tried dropping the anchor to slow down the drift, but one anchor wasn't enough. So we dropped another anchor, and with both anchors dragging we slowed down enough to catch a mess of fluke.

There's a certain knack to hooking fish while drifting. Some species will grab a bait and get hooked without any effort on the angler's part. But most of the time, when you feel a bite you should let out slack line and give the fish a few seconds to swallow the bait. When using a conventional-type reel, you should keep it in free spool so that you can let out line in a split second. With a spinning reel the bail should be opened, for the same reason.

On a slow drift in deep water you can often keep the

Florida has many fish, like this grouper, for drift fishermen (or fisherwomen).

sinker bouncing under the boat. If the water is shallow or the wind or tide fairly strong, you should let out more slack line so that the sinker and bait move some distance behind the boat.

In recent years party boats and private boats fishing for bluefish have found that they can take these fish while drifting and chumming with ground bunker or menhaden. You can also drift and chum for such fish as mackerel, bonito and false albacore. Here it is usually best if the boat moves sideways with the wind and tide and the hook, baited with a piece of butterfish, menhaden or a small bait fish, is let out in the chum slick without a sinker.

My favorite method of drift-fishing is to cast into a school of fish with a light spinning outfit. In this case, of course, you have to locate a school feeding on top and then cast a lure into it. This can be done with most species which feed on top and chase bait fish. Such fish as bluefish, weakfish, striped bass, channel bass, bonito, snook and tarpon can often be caught this way. Naturally, the type of tackle you use will depend on the size of the fish. Light spin outfits are used for small fish, while surf squidding or popping sticks can be used for larger fish such as striped bass, channel bass, tarpon and school tuna.

One of the easiest ways to fish a bonefish flat in the Florida Keys is by drifting. You merely run your outboard boat up on a flat during the incoming tide and let the wind or tide move you slowly until you spot a bonefish. Then you cast a bucktail jig or other bonefish lure in front of the fish. It's a lot less work than poling the boat or wading a flat.

Casting while drifting also produces fish on many occasions when they are down deep. Here you use a jig such as the bucktail type or a chrome-plated diamond jig. If the water isn't too deep and if the tide and wind are not too strong, you merely let the jig down to the bottom under the boat. When you feel it hit bottom you start jigging the lure up and down as the boat drifts slowly. If the wind or tide is strong try casting the jig ahead of the moving boat to allow slack line to develop. This permits the lure to sink toward the bottom. A light spinning outfit with an 8- or 10-lb. test line is best for such fishing.

One of the best ways to catch that big tarpon in Florida is to drift with live bait fish such as mullet, pinfish or catfish. This can be done by attaching a cork float about 10 ft. above the hook and letting it out in the current. For best results, your boat should stay some distance away from the cork float.

At Boca Grande Pass and Captiva Pass on Florida's west coast they drift for tarpon using a blue crab for bait and tie a sinker weighing anywhere from 3 to 8 oz. about 8 ft. above the hook. This sinker is tied on with light line so that it breaks off the line when the tarpon first leaps.

At Bahía Honda in the Florida Keys the tarpon fishermen drift with the tide toward the bridge and cast plugs or spoons into schools of rolling tarpon. This, of course, can also be done in other areas where tarpon are showing on top.

If you want to catch a big amberjack in Florida waters try drifting over the reefs with a live mullet, grunt, pinfish, snapper or blue runner on the hook. Here it's a good idea to chum with ground fish or pieces of fish to attract the amberjack. When they are sighted or believed to be in the area you let out the live bait fish about 40 or 50 ft. behnd the boat as it drifts along. If you try this sort of fishing use sturdy tackle and fairly heavy lines. Amberjack are tough scrappers and are difficult to hold on light tackle.

Some eye-opening catches of big striped bass have also been made by the live-bait drift-fishing method. Capt. Dick Lema of Galilee, Rhode Island, fishes this way on his charter boat with live eels and mostly at night. The eels are drifted naturally over rocks and reefs, where big striped bass are known to lie in wait for such tidbits. The angler casts the live eel, hooked through the jaw, about 50 feet from the boat and lets out slack line. When he feels the eel stop or move away very fast he feeds some more slack line. Then, a few seconds later, he reels up the slack line, and when it tightens he

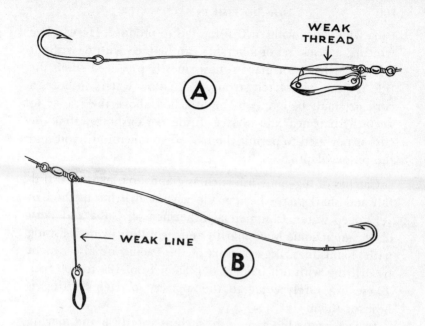

Rig "A" is popular with drift fishermen seeking tarpon. When a tarpon jumps, the sinker comes off. Rig "B" is for bottom drifting over rocky areas. If the sinker gets caught it breaks off.

comes back with the rod to set the hook. Most of the stripers hooked by this drifting method run from 30 to 60 lbs. in weight.

Drift-fishing practiced in deeper offshore waters also accounts for big-game fish at times. When sailfishing, for example, if the fish aren't showing or refuse to take a trolled bait, try drifting with a live blue runner. At first, you can try letting the blue runner down to about 10 or 12 feet below the surface. If this fails you let your bait fish swim down to 40 or 50 feet below the surface.

Tuna fishermen also know that drifting often catches big

tuna when anchoring or trolling fail to produce. Here, a live whiting, a mackerel or a herring can be used with or without a float. Drifting for giant tuna is mostly practiced when the tide is slack or not too strong. In shallow waters inshore, a cork or small balloon can be attached above the leader to keep the bait near the surface. In deeper offshore waters the cork is not used to permit the bait to go down until you find the proper depth.

Catches of big-game fish such as giant tuna, marlin, sword-fish and sharks have been made via the drifting method in very deep water. Commercial fishermen off Cuba and Peru have caught some huge marlin and swordfish by drift-fishing with hand lines. Big-eye tuna of the Pacific are also caught by drifting with fish baits at depths of from 100 to 300 feet. These fish rarely come to the surface, so deep drifting is best for them.

In fact, many big game fish, such as swordfish and marlin, are believed to feed more often well below the surface than on top. When swordfish are found on the surface they are rarely feeding but usually resting. Their stomachs are often full and they aren't too interested in additional food, so it's difficult to make them strike. Also, swordfishing on the sur-face requires calm water conditions because these fish are sighted first before the bait is put out.

Generally, the big-game angler who resorts to deep drift-ing stands an excellent chance of hooking a big fish in the deeper offshore waters. He also spends more time actually fishing and less time cruising around, burning up gas and straining his eyes for signs of fish. He can also fish on days when the water is too choppy or rough for sighting the fins of swordfish or marlin.

All in all, drift-fishing is a versatile and deadly method for almost all kinds of salt-water game fish. Try it as often as possible this coming fishing season. If you're like me you'll spend more and more time drift-fishing and less and less time fishing at anchor or trolling.

9

CATCH THEM AT NIGHT

The great majority of salt-water anglers go out during the daytime and rarely venture forth at night. But today more and more anglers are discovering that plenty of fish and good sport can also be had at night. In fact, if you are interested in big fish which are found near shore, your chances are much better fishing at night than during the daytime.

But night fishing in salt water offers many other advantages besides that of catching big fish. There are fewer anglers and less competition, so you have more elbow room. You don't have to worry about sunburn, and often during the summer the wind dies at sundown, so the water is usually calmer at night than during the middle of the day—an important point to consider if you are subject to seasickness. Also, during the summer months it is cooler at the seashore or on the water at night. Finally, you can fool the fish easier at night than during the day. They can't see the hook, leader or line, and they can't examine a lure too closely.

Fish of many kinds—both game species and bottom species —can be caught at night from boats, bridges, piers, and the shore and in the surf. Bay fishermen go after striped bass, bluefish and weakfish in northern waters from small boats. Striped bass, especially, can be caught around bridge pilings, in deep holes, along edges of sand or rock bars at night with lures such as small plugs and bucktails. Other anglers go after striped bass using a float and putting a sandworm or blood-worm on a hook and floating this out in the current.

After dark, weakfish are most co-operative when you are fishing in bays where they are found. The usual bait used for them is a sandworm, piece of squid, shrimp or shedder crab fished on the bottom with a sinker just heavy enough to hold bottom.

Another fish which often bites at night is the bluefish. In fact, bigger catches of these fish are usually taken chumming at night than during the daytime, for bigger bluefish seem to bite after dark. Sometimes common bonito show up in the chum at night and are also caught.

Bottom fishermen fishing from boats, piers or bridges at night often catch porgies and croakers in the North and snappers and groupers in the South. Those who like to catch conger eels or the common eels will also find the nighttime best for them. In fact, during the daytime these fish often vanish, but after dark they reappear in large numbers.

If you want to fool a snook or a tarpon in Florida or in other tropical waters, you can't pick a better time to fish than at night. Using surface and underwater plugs and jigs or live bait fish, you'll often fool trophy snook and tarpon, which frequent passes and bridges in many southern areas.

Sharks—if you want to catch them—are also bolder and more numerous at night, when they come closer to shore and to the surface in search of food. Then they can be caught from boats, bridges, piers and the shore.

But the guy who really collects big dividends from night fishing is the surf angler. If you want to fool fish like the striped bass, you'll discover that the time put in fishing at night is worth the effort.

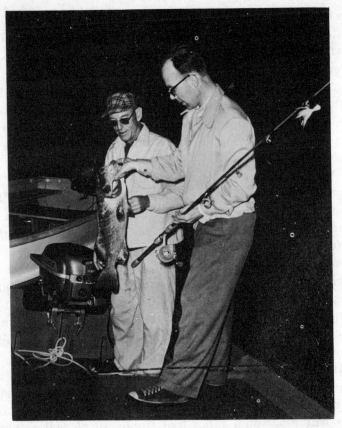

Many fish bite at night on both natural baits and jigs. This one was taken in the Bahamas by Ray Ovington, outdoor writer.

I recall one August evening some years ago when I was fishing the Cape Cod Canal with my brother and another angler. About an hour before dark we had walked out to the big breakwater on the north end of the canal and were trying for the stripers which were fairly plentiful in the big ditch at that time. Using an underwater plug I cast out and reeled in. As the plug came into view near shore I saw a striper of about 15 lbs. following behind it. Then the fish veered off without hitting the lure. On several casts after that stripers would follow our lures up to the rocks but wouldn't hit. We tried working the lures in various ways, and we tried everything in our bags, including various surface and underwater plugs, eelskins, feather and bucktail lures—even metal squids. Still no luck. However, as soon as it got dark we started to get action with eelskins and after a couple of hours had nine nice stripers lying on the rocks.

This was just one instance where night fishing for stripers paid off. I've had many other similar experiences. In fact, during some twenty-five years of fishing for stripers from Cape Cod to New Jersey, I've caught at least three stripers at night for every one I've caught during the daytime. I know that most of the veteran beach and jetty jockeys along the Atlantic Coast will back me up. These men have learned the hard way—after many thousands of casts and weary hours and days of plugging—that the striper is a night owl. If you want to get your share of fish you have to miss plenty of sleep.

Night fishing in the surf is almost a must in highly populated areas, especially from Memorial Day to Labor Day. In many areas, most surf anglers are forced to fish at night in the summer. During the daytime there are too many bathers and they chase the surf anglers away from the best spots. Luckily, in the case of the striped bass, this isn't such a hardship. Since they bite best at night during the summer months most anglers I know don't bother going out until well after dark. Then they usually fish hard until the early morning hours or even until daybreak.

Novice surf anglers or those who have never done much night fishing often wonder how it is possible to locate, hook and land fish in the surf on a dark night. Many have asked me such questions as the following: How do you know where to fish? How can you cast at night? How do you land the fish?

It's true that problems and conditions which are easily coped with during the daytime are often more difficult on a dark night. Yet it's surprising how soon you become used to casting, hooking and landing fish at night and enjoying it as much or even more than during the daytime.

The big question that arises with respect to surf fishing at night is how to locate the fish. If you are lucky enough to have a friend who can tip you off, that's a big help. Tackle dealers and outdoors columns in newspapers often tell you the general area to fish. Actually, no one can predict in advance which specific spots will produce a temperamental fish such as the striped bass, because they move around too much and bite best under conditions which change from day to day.

At night there are no birds to guide you, but if you see birds or fish feeding off the beach during the daytime there is a good chance that they will work inshore at dusk or after dark. Schools of bait fish will often lie off the beach during the day, but at night they tend to work inshore to escape the game fish, and, of course, the game fish will often follow them in. If you arrive after dark you can pick up the bait fish in your light when they are hugging the shoreline.

Sometimes you can see fish breaking water, especially on moonlit nights, and sometimes you can even hear them. But most of the time they do not show and this is where a knowledge of the shoreline pays off. In order to pick up this knowledge, you must study or fish the same spots during the day, noting the depth of the water, the formation and location of sand bars or rocks and the action of the waves and currents. The same spots which produced fish during the daytime will usually produce at night. Such knowledge will also prevent you from casting into shallow areas or rocks when you fish at night. Another hazard, during the summer months, is the lifelines that are strung out from the shore to protect swimmers in bathing areas. Quite a few jetty anglers have hooked into such lines and for a few exciting moments thought they had nailed a record striper.

If you fish the Long Island and New Jersey beaches near New York City, most of your night fishing will be done from

Night fishing produces many a big striper like these, caught on Dick Lema's boat. Standing in the white shirt is Jerry Sylvester, well-known surf angler, who has spent thousands of hours fishing at night along the Narragansett shores of Rhode Island.

the rock jetties and breakwaters commonly found there. Although some anglers fish from the beach between the jetties, best results are usually obtained by going out on the structures.

Some jetties are considered better than others since they produce more fish throughout the season. The better ones are usually located near deep holes or bar formations and rips which provide good feeding spots for stripers and other fish. Most jetties have a fairly strong current at the end and along the sides. At high tide and with a heavy sea it may not be possible to fish at the extreme end of the jetty. So under these circumstances you will have to fish from the sides. It pays to make an occasional cast toward the front of the jetty and then to work the lure as close to the rocks as possible without fouling. When the tide drops to more than half-out you can usually go out to the end. Here, the usual procedure is to cast in a semicircle around the tip of the jetty.

If I plan to fish more than one jetty, I usually start making my casts along one side as soon as I get out past the first line of breakers; then I walk up a few feet and make another cast into deeper water; and so on until I get to the end, where I "fan" my casts in a semicircle. Then I work back along the opposite side toward shore. In this way I cover most of the water around the jetty. However, if it is low tide and there isn't much water along the sides of the jetty I usually head right out to the end and cast into the deeper water. However, it's tough work trying to fish more than one or two jetties so most anglers pick one and stay there for two or three hours.

Casting at night can be more troublesome than during the daytime. The spool on a conventional-type surf reel should be filled with a line that is neither too heavy nor too light. A 30- or 36-lb. test, braided nylon line is about right. A white, tan or other light-colored line is easier to see in the dark. When using a spinning reel, you have to make sure that the line is not fouled around some part of the reel. This is especially true on windy nights.

When actually casting, don't try for distance. At night you can't see the lure traveling through the air, so you won't have any idea where it will strike the water. Aim high rather than low and stop the cast soon after the lure loses momentum and starts dropping. If you get a backlash or line snarl, strip plenty of line off the spool and make sure there are no snarls remaining before you reel it back on again. This is very important if you want to prevent trouble on the next cast.

At night, hooking and landing a fish from a level sand beach isn't much harder than in the daytime. If the fish runs down the beach you can easily follow it without a light. A fish hooked along a rocky shore or from a jetty is another story. Here you'll often need the help of a light to follow and work the fish into the rocks where you can reach it.

Unless the water is calm, a gaff is usually needed to land a fish from a jetty or breakwater. The gaff should have a long handle and I find that painting the gaff white helps to locate it quickly when you lay it down on the rocks. It is a good idea to fish a jetty with another angler so you can be of mutual assistance. Then, unless both of you hook into a fish at the same time, one man is always free to use the light and gaff the fish. It is also safer to fish a jetty with another man.

Speaking of safety, night fishing requires much more caution than daytime angling. Jetties and rocks which can be navigated with ease during the daytime can cause trouble at night. Ice-creepers or wading sandals worn under your feet to provide a grip on slippery moss-covered rocks are a must. Waves are more of a threat at night since you don't always see them coming and a rising tide must be watched closely so that you don't get trapped out on a jetty or rock. You have to study the rocks and work out a plan of action for landing a fish *before* you make the first cast, otherwise, in the excitement which follows, you may take a nasty spill. Above all, night fishing calls for a slower pace than daytime fishing. Take it easy when casting, walking or landing a fish and you generally won't have any trouble.

Which lures are best for night fishing? For striped bass give me a rigged eel every time. You just can't beat the "snakes" when there are good-sized stripers around. If you plan to go out at night from June to November, you should always carry these reliable bass killers. Surface plugs and underwater plugs are also popular lures. Metal squids and spoons are not too good for night fishing in the surf, but they should be carried if you plan to fish around dusk or daybreak. Most of the artificial lures bring more strikes if they are retrieved somewhat slower than they are during the daytime.

Natural baits often produce at night. During the summer months you can't beat shedder crabs and skimmer or sea clams in the surf. The blue-claw shedders are not as good for surf fishing as the calico or lady crabs. Seaworms, squid and the sand bugs found in the sand under the waves are also good striper baits at times. At night, the bait fisherman may be bothered a bit more by crabs and other pests, such as dogfish and skates, but by bringing along plenty of bait and using a cork to keep it off the bottom it is possible to have good fishing.

For me, surf casting at night equals any fishing experienced during the daytime. Some of my most memorable surf-fishing trips have been at night. Hooking and landing a good-sized striper in the moonlight gives me a greater thrill than landing the same fish when the sun is shining. Even on dark nights surf fishing has a quality all of its own. There is a great deal of mystery and suspense involved in hooking something big on the end of your line on a black night.

10

PARTY-BOAT FISHING PAYS OFF!

In fishing, as in everything else, tastes differ and each salt-water angler prefers one type of fishing above all others. Some guys like to seek big game in offshore waters. Others like the surf and spend their time trying for stripers, channel bass and weakfish. Many go for bottom fishing from boats, shore piers and bridges. Still others, like myself, believe every kind of fishing has something to offer. I enjoy any type of salt-water fishing just so long as it offers some kind of action, fun and a chance of catching a few fish.

Naturally, almost every type of salt-water fishing will fit the above requirements on certain days. But the type which comes closest to offering action, fun and fish on most occasions is party-boat fishing. Party boats are also called open-party boats, open boats, deep-sea boats, drift boats, ground-fishing boats and bottom-fishing boats. They leave at a set time from many ports along the Atlantic, Pacific and Gulf coasts.

They are called open boats because they are open to the public, which means that you don't have to charter them or reserve a place. Just walk on and grab a spot along the rail. They offer the great advantage of being available whenever you're in the mood to go fishing. You don't have to make reservations weeks or months ahead of time as you have to do with charter boats. You can wait until the last minute, make up your mind and hop on the boat just before it sails.

Of course, if you want a certain spot it's better to arrive an hour or so earlier. Most party boats leave anywhere from 5:00 A.M. to 10:00 A.M. and return in the late afternoon. A full day's trip will give you anywhere from six to ten hours on the water. Actually the time spent fishing will be less since it often takes up to two hours running time to reach the fishing grounds. In some areas, such as Florida, there are also half-day trips with the boats leaving about 9:00 A.M., returning at 1:00 P.M., leaving again in the early afternoon and returning about 5:00 P.M. In some places there are also night fishing trips from about 7:00 P.M. to a short time after midnight.

The cost? Anywhere from $4.00 to $12.00, depending on the size of the boat, where the fishing is being done, the type of fishing being done and the port you sail from. The smaller boats and boats making short trips charge less than the larger ones making long trips. Those that leave early for distant grounds and return late, charge more than the boats that spend less time on the water or fish only half a day. But whatever the cost you can be sure it's a bargain compared to cost of renting or chartering a boat.

What boat should you choose? It all depends on what you want. In ports with only one or two party boats you obviously have little choice. In other ports like Sheepshead Bay, New York, you have almost fifty party boats to choose from. If you don't mind getting up early you can take one of the 5:00 A.M. boats. If you like to sleep you can make one of the later boats. A small boat is less crowded and you'll get better service and attention from the captain and crew. On the

Party boat anglers leave the Elmar *with their catch at Sheeps-head Bay, N. Y. It may include porgies, sea bass, flounders, fluke, blackfish, bluefish, mackerel, albacore or bonito. During the winter months cod, whiting, haddock, pollock and ling or hake are taken.*

larger boats you have better accommodations—benches, enclosed cabins, small snack bars, etc. The bigger boats are usually faster and more seaworthy and you take less of a beating in rough waters. However, most party boats are run by capable skippers and several trips on various craft will give you a real idea of what they offer.

More important is to find out if ocean conditions are suitable for the day's fishing—and if the fish are running. I find it a good idea to go down to the fishing docks in the afternoon a day before I plan to go out. Then I watch the returning party boats and check with the anglers on how the fish were biting, how the water conditions were, what kind of fish were running, etc. If the bags are heavy with fish, that's a tip-off that the next day may repeat, provided, of course, that weather conditions remain the same. So the next morning, before you step on the boat, check the weather report. If it sounds O.K. you can go aboard with some assurance that the chances of catching fish are good.

Another thing to check is what kind of fish the boat you go on is after. Some boats concentrate on a single species; others take anything that comes. If you want to catch, let's say, fluke or summer flounders don't make the mistake of boarding a boat which is going after porgies or sea bass. Ask the captain or mate what fish they are going after before you go aboard. Naturally, in areas such as Florida the catches are so mixed that no species really predominates in the day's fishing. In this case you just have to settle for the fish you get.

Naturally, party boats are more crowded on weekends and holidays than on weekdays. If you want more elbow room you'll do better if you take the day off and go out on a weekday .

You will have a choice of spots on the boat itself if you arrive early. Many veteran party boaters prefer the stern of the boat. You're closer to the water there and it's usually a productive spot. Most fish head into the running tide so that when the boat is anchored they will hit the lines at the stern first. It doesn't make as much difference if the boat is drifting. In this case it is better to be on the side where the lines move away from the boat. On crowded boats this isn't always possible, so many captains often alternate the drift so that half the anglers don't fish the entire day with the lines running under the boat.

Party boats come in various sizes from small 30-footers to big 100-foot jobs like this one. They all offer safe and economical fishing.

Most party boats have tackle for rent but these outfits may be heavier and stiffer than some anglers prefer. It's best to bring your own. The rod you should use depends on the depth of the water, the strength of currents and tides, the type of bottom being fished, the sinker weight required and the size of the fish being caught. For small fish in shallow or medium depths and sinkers not over 4 or 5 oz. you can use the lighter flounder- or weakfish-type rods.

The favorite party-boat rod is the so-called boat rod, which comes in lengths from 5 to 8 ft. over-all. Shorter, lighter rods are for smaller fish in shallow water. Longer, heavier rods are better for larger fish in deep water. Hollow and solid glass rods are the most widely used.

Some anglers also use surf rods on party boats. They work fairly well for big fish in deep water, and their length helps to keep the line away from the boat and aids in bringing a fish over the rail. They are also useful if you have to cast a rig or bait some distance from the boat. But casting on a crowded party boat is hazardous and therefore discouraged. The trouble with surf rods is that the butts are too long and get in the way and the rods are a bit on the heavy side.

Spinning rods and reels aren't too good for party boat fishing unless everyone is using them or unless the boat isn't too crowded. Then you can use the lighter spinning rods and lines. But on crowded boats and for deep fishing with heavy sinkers the heaviest spinning rods and lines are required. You can't play a fish too well on a crowded party boat. If it runs to the left or right there will be one mess of lines. You have to bring a big fish to the gaff without too much fuss. There are usually only one or two men working with gaffs. So in the long run, a regular boat rod or conventional-type surf rod is better to use on a party boat than a spinning outfit. Of course, when you are going for fish which are taken on top with lures or live bait, spinning rods are often in order.

The reel you use should, of course, suit the rod. For lighter conventional rods almost any salt-water reel holding up to 150 yds. of line is suitable. For heavier rods, reels holding 200 or 300 yds. are preferred, especially in deep water. When drift-fishing in very deep water an even larger reel holding up to 400 or 500 yds. of line may be needed.

When selecting lines you have a choice of linen, braided nylon or braided dacron. They're all used, but in recent years many have turned to monofilament. The latter is strong, fools wary fish and stands abuse around mussels, wrecks, rocks, coral reefs and similar hazards. You lose fewer rigs, hook more fish and land more of them with mono lines.

The test of the line will depend on the outfit you use, the fish being sought and the bottom being fished. For light outfits, small fish and clear bottoms, lines from 20 to 30 lbs. can be used. With heavy outfits, big fish and bottoms covered with obstructions, lines testing from 30 to 60 lbs. are better.

The basic party-boat rig in northern waters is the "deep sea" rig. A bank or diamond sinker is tied to the end of the line. One hook on a short snell or leader is tied just above the sinker, then another one is tied above the first hook just high enough to clear it. If you are going after cod, haddock, pollack, longer leaders and larger hooks such as 7/0 or 8/0 are used. For smaller fish such as scup or porgies and tautog or blackfish, shorter leaders and 1/0 or 2/0 hooks are required.

In southern waters party-boat anglers prefer the sliding sinker rig. Here you slip an egg-shaped sinker on the end of the line. The sinker has a hole running through the center so that the sinker can slide up and down. Next you tie a barrel swivel on the end of the line, after which you tie your leader and hook to the other end of the barrel swivel. The swivel acts as a stop and the sinker can slide or the fish can pull the line without feeling the weight of the lead. The principle is similar to that of the surfman's "fish-finder" rig described and illustrated in Chapter 4.

Sinker weights will depend on the depth of the water, the strength of the current or tide and the method of fishing. Most party boaters use 6- or 8-oz. sinkers in shallow or medium depths. For deeper water and strong currents 10 or 12 oz. is better. Under extreme conditions you may need sinkers weighing close to a pound.

Hooks will range from No. 1 or slightly smaller on up to No. 12/0 for big fish. The O'Shaughnessy, Sproat and Eagle Claw patterns are the most widely used. Special patterns for certain fish include the Carlisle for fluke or summer flounder and for silver hake or whiting; Virginia hooks are used for blackfish or tautog and sheepshead; while Chestertown hooks are best for winter flounders.

It is understood that on most party boats the bait is supplied at no extra charge. In northern waters the most commonly used baits are skimmer clams, squid and small fish. In southern waters you'll find mostly cut mullet or shrimp. There is usually plenty of bait available but it is limited to one or two kinds. Of course, there's nothing to stop you from buying your own bait and carrying it on board. The more baits you have, the better your chances of appealing to some kind of fish.

The fish you'll catch on party boats will depend on the area being fished, the season and the species most plentiful at the time. In northern waters the season gets under way in early spring with cod, haddock, pollack, silver hake or whiting, tautog or blackfish and winter flounders. In the summer and early fall you get porgies or scup, sea bass, summer flounder or fluke. Then it's back to winter species such as cod and haddock again.

In the years when bluefish are plentiful party boats also go after these fish. They also hook albacore, bonito and mackerel if these fish are around in numbers.

Farther south off Virginia and North Carolina you get some of these species mentioned above as well as hardhead or croakers, spot, sheepshead and at times cobia, black drum, and red snappers.

In Florida and in the Gulf of Mexico the majority of party boats seek snappers, especially big red snappers, and many kinds of grunts. Groupers of various kinds are also caught. These boats also snag amberjack, barracuda, triggerfish, angelfish, and a host of other species. Anglers fishing from party boats have also hauled in lobsters, big sea eels, turtles, sharks, rays and even small tuna.

Skippers who run party boats know the location of most of the fishing grounds in their areas. The best spots include sunken wrecks, mussel and other shellfish beds, rocky bottoms, coral reefs and the so-called banks. These are plateaus or shallow areas in normally deeper water where marine life abounds and bottom fish gather to feed. In northern waters these banks are famous for the codfish and haddock they attract, while in the south the red-snapper banks attract commercial and sports fishermen.

Whether you anchor or drift is up to the skipper. He has to take the weather, water, tide conditions and the fish you are after into consideration. Generally when fishing small wrecks, confined mussel and rock bottoms anchoring is best, but when fishing broad banks, drifting is usually better. The fish may be spread out or congregated in a small area, so drifting gets better results. Most bottom fish can be caught while anchored or drifting. About the only exception is the tautog or blackfish, which likes to stick close to obstructions and takes its time about swallowing a bait. This is also true of the winter flounder. Slow drifting, with the boat barely moving, may get them, but too fast a drift doesn't give them a chance to get at the bait. In fact, if the tide or wind is too strong the boat will drift too fast to get the bait down to the bottom. And even if it does get there it moves too fast for many bottom fish.

Whether anchored or drifting it's important to feel bottom at all times. Let out slack so that the sinker bounces on the bottom, but don't leave too much of a belly in your line or you won't be able to feel a bite.

Fishing from a party boat can be a lot of fun. You may rub shoulders with a plumber on one side and a banker on the other. When you first get on the boat you may be strangers, but by the time the boat docks again you are chatting like old friends. You meet a lot of regular guys and make new friends.

Unfortunately, on almost every trip there are one or two bad eggs who try to spoil it for the rest. Many anglers fishing from party boats for the first time don't know what is expected of them. Others may be veteran party boaters who just don't give a damn for anyone else.

There's the guy who hits the bottle too often and becomes a menace to himself and everyone else. He tangles lines, slips on the deck, bumps into other anglers, tries to make trouble and is just a plain nuisance.

Or there's the kind who uses the four letter words despite the fact that there are kids and women on board within hearing distance.

Or the character who insists on casting over the heads of nearby anglers. If he likes casting so much or thinks it is the only way to get fish, then why not do it from a beach, jetty or private boat? A crowded boat is no place for casting. You can flip your bait out from the side of the boat a sufficient distance.

Then we have the griper who growls about the bait, the weather, the kind of fish caught, their size, the location being fished, tangled lines, other fishermen, etc. This fellow usually wants the boat moved every ten minutes. Some griping is acceptable, of course, if not overdone. It's only human but it doesn't solve the problem. If you notice anything really wrong, go up and speak to the captain or mate. But don't sound off for hours and spoil the fun of everyone else near you.

Sometimes the skipper or crew may be to blame for unsatisfactory conditions. On too many party boats the crew fishes instead of catering to the wants of the anglers. They fish to make extra money by selling the fish to unlucky anglers or to the market when they return to port. Naturally a crew member concentrating on his fishing can't always be available to gaff fish, untangle lines, make up rigs for novices, bring more bait or do any of the other things which help to make a good party boat.

No captain can guarantee fish on a given day, for too many things can happen over which he has no control. Individual fishermen also vary in ability and know-how. Some catch on quickly and get their share of fish. Others are slow or stubborn and refuse to take advice. So on almost every trip there are some anglers who catch few or no fish even though the other anglers have a sackful.

Party-boat fishing is a more sociable type of fishing than other salt-water methods. You have to be a good sport and take crowded conditions, line tangles, rough water and poor fishing as they come. If you make enough party-boat trips the odds are greatly in your favor. You are practically guaranteed action, fun and fish on the majorty of your trips.

One other attraction on many party boats is the daily pool. Here, whoever feels like it can chip in a specified amount, usually around a dollar or fifty cents. Then whoever catches the biggest fish takes the accumulated total. This makes for friendly competition and a lot of joking as one angler beats out another with a heavier fish. On weekends such pools have often run up to a couple of hundred dollars for the lucky (or skillful) angler. Yep, party-boat fishing pays off in more ways than most types of salt-water fishing.

11

PIER, BRIDGE AND JETTY FISHING

With the popularity of salt-water fishing increasing, one big problem is how to accommodate the growing army of anglers. With more and more hotels, apartments, bathing beaches and private homes being built along our shores, fishing space is at a premium. One way this problem is being solved is by building fishing piers into bays, sounds and the ocean. This is being done on a grand scale in some states, such as North Carolina and Florida.

But in other states—mostly in the New England and Middle Atlantic area—fishing piers are scarce. New York State, for example, has only one pier along its long ocean front on Long Island—that one at Coney Island. But along the rest of the 100 or so miles to Montauk Point there isn't a single pier running out into the ocean.

There are so many advantages in pier fishing that it is a wonder that more aren't built to accommodate salt-water anglers. Pier fishing provides fun for everyone. It is also a poor man's sport and a family pastime, for you can fish daily at small cost: most fishing piers are free, while others charge a small fee ranging from twenty-five cents to a dollar or so. You can fish at your own convenience, for you can arrive

123

and leave whenever you please. No time is wasted running out to the fishing grounds and back in a boat. You don't have to worry about rough water, strong winds or seasickness. Many piers are open twenty-four hours a day.

Piers are usually made from wood, but some are constructed from steel or concrete. Some are low and close to the water while others are high. Most of them run only a few hundred feet in length but some run 1,000 feet or more. Some piers have benches, rest rooms, restaurants and faucets with running water for cleaning fish. Still others have tackle stores where you can buy bait or tackle or rent a rod and reel. It all adds up to safe, comfortable fishing, appealing to all ages and both sexes.

Of course, not all piers offer equally good fishing. The best ones are built over grounds which attract fish from time to time. The location of a pier is very important, so if you have a choice choose the pier which has produced fish in past years. Pier fishing is generally best when fish are schooled up and feeding or migrating. This usually occurs during the spring and fall months. But some areas also provide good fishing during the summer and even during the winter months.

Almost any kind of fishing tackle can be used for pier fishing, but boat rods and heavier spinning rods are preferred. Surf outfits are also good if you have to cast any distance. Light spinning rods are used by those casting with lures for the smaller species, but no matter which outfit you use, it should be strong enough to handle sinkers up to 6 or 8 oz. for bottom fishing. It should be able to handle the fish being sought, and it should be strong enough to haul in smaller species without breaking the line.

Pier fishermen use many of the same rigs for bottom fishing as those described in Chapter 4. Another popular rig is a float or bobber attached anywhere from 4 to 10 feet above

Pier fishing is popular with everybody, especially youngsters, who often catch more fish than the older anglers. Almost every large coastal city in Florida has one or more fishing piers.

the hook. A clincher sinker is attached to the leader between the float and the hook, which is baited with a live bait fish, seaworm, crab, shrimp, piece of squid or other salt-water bait and is drifted out with the current. The advantage of this rig is that the tide can carry it out some distance and you cover more territory.

Many fish, such as striped bass, porgies, blackfish or tautog, croakers, sheepshead, snappers, grunt and groupers will be found right under the pier among the piles. They come to feed on the mussels, barnacles, seaweed, crabs and other marine life found there. But even game fish may swim by and stop to feed on the smaller fish which take refuge under a pier.

Certain species, such as striped bass, channel bass, bluefish, weakfish and sea trout, will often be found in the shallow water near shore or in the surf. Other species prefer the deeper water near the end of the pier.

If the fish aren't biting directly under the pier try casting away from the structure into deeper water at the point. Or do the same thing along the sides. If you know of a deep hole, a rocky bottom, or a mussel or oyster bar near the pier try to reach that with your bait or lure.

Pier fishing is often good at night and then it's a good idea to fish near a light. You not only see what you are doing but the light attracts smaller bait fish and they in turn attract the larger game fish. Some anglers bring their own lights and suspend them under the pier. Another good approach to bridge fishing is to chum from the pier by tossing out crushed clams, mussels, crabs or pieces of fish, squid and shrimp. You can also fill a chum pot or mesh bag with such stuff and lower it on a string to the bottom under the pier.

One problem in pier fishing is landing a fish from the greater height. With small fish it's not much of a job—you just reel them in or haul them in hand over hand if the line is strong enough. With bigger fish you may need a long-handled gaff. This can be used from piers which are close to the water. From higher piers you can sometimes walk a fish up to shore and than gaff or beach it. Another device for landing fish is a grappling hook with several prongs on it.

This is lowered on a strong line and is used to snag a fish in the mouth or gills. Some piers also have large scoop nets with a wide wire hoop which can be lowered under a big fish.

But despite the difficulties, many large fish, such as tarpon, cobia, channel bass, striped bass, grouper and sharks, are landed from piers from time to time.

Somewhat similar to pier fishing is bridge fishing. There are many bridges running over salt-water bays, rivers and inlets which can be fished. Others are dangerous because of heavy auto traffic and lack of space for anglers to stand. Florida, no doubt, has more bridges where fishing is done than any other state. But almost every coastal state has a few bridges which can be fished.

Bridges, of course, cross from one point of land to another and in so doing cover all the different depths of the body of water they cross. Bridges vary in length and construction and height above the water. Some are low and close to the water while others are high. Those that are high above the water are best suited to fishing with bait, while the lower ones can often be worked with artificial lures.

Fishing under a bridge will naturally vary with the location and the type of water which flows under it. Like piers, bridges also attract fish because of the growth of mussels and barnacles on their supports. But bridges also help create strong currents and tidal rips since they often interfere with the flow of the water. As a result many game fish lurk alongside or behind the bridge supports waiting for smaller fish to swim by or get trapped in the swirling currents.

When fishing a strange bridge it's a good idea to walk along the rails on both sides and study the currents and depths. Try to spot fish breaking or feeding below. Look for concentrations of small bait fish. The stage of the tide often plays an important part when you are fishing from a bridge. The fishing may be good on one side during the incoming tide and on the opposite side on the outgoing tide. The change of the tide is often a trigger which starts fish feeding. Try to be on the bridge just before this happens.

Bridge fishermen can use the same tackle as that used from piers: boat rods, spinning rods and surf rods. The length and weight of the rod, the strength of the line and the size of the reel will depend on the fish you are going after. If you are seeking striped bass, snook, or tarpon you can use medium tackle. But if you go after sharks or jewfish you need heavy stuff.

The same goes for the rigs, hooks, sinkers and baits used. Again, these will depend on the fish you are seeking at the time. For bottom fishing the high-leader rig described in Chapter 4 is often good for bluefish, striped bass, weakfish, channel bass and other species. With a second smaller hook attached lower you can also catch blackfish or tautog, porgies, sea bass, flounders, croakers and eels.

One good way to fish from a bridge is to bounce the sinker along the bottom, letting the rig drift farther and farther away from the bridge. In order to do this you need a sinker just heavy enough to hit bottom and stay there for awhile but light enough to move when the rod tip is lifted.

You can also cast out to a spot where you think the fish may be present. Here, too, mussel beds, rocky patches, oyster beds and deep holes and channels are usually most productive.

Or you can try using a float or bobber above a hook without a sinker and let it drift out away from the bridge in the tide. This method can be used for fish such as striped bass, weakfish, sea trout, snook, tarpon and sharks. For the latter three fish a live bait fish often works best.

Many anglers also use artificial lures such as jigs, spoons, metal squids and plugs from a bridge. You can cast these and reel them in by keeping the rod tip down. Jigs can be lowered under the bridge to the bottom and worked up and down alongside the piles.

A popular method on some bridges, such as those found at the Florida Keys is to "walk" lures like the jig or plug alongside the bridge. Here you should let out enough line to get the lure down to the proper depth, then start walking slowly to make the lure work.

When you hook a fish from a bridge you have to be careful in fighting it because many fish, such as snook and striped bass, will try to foul your line around the bridge supports. They must be kept from doing this since the rough concrete or mussels will quickly cut your line.

You will have the same problems in landing fish from a bridge as from a pier. Most bridges are too high above the water to allow the use of a gaff, so you have to resort to grapple hooks and hoop nets which can be lowered under the fish. Or you can try to tow a big fish toward one end of the bridge and then beach him. Small fish, of course, can be hauled in quickly by simply reeling them in.

Finally there are various jetties and breakwaters which can be fished by salt-water anglers. Thousands of jetties and breakwaters have been built along the Atlantic and Gulf coasts to protect inlets and beaches from erosion. Most of the jetties are short, running out a few hundred feet or so. But some of the larger breakwaters may extend a mile or two into the ocean. These are usually flat and can be navigated easily. Some of the breakwaters along the Gulf Coast are concrete-capped and offer fairly safe and comfortable fishing platforms.

Jetties are usually made of big granite boulders, which soon attract mussels and barnacles, crabs, shrimp, small fish and other marine life. These in turn attract the larger game fish which lurk around the rocks and wait for an easy meal.

Jetties and breakwaters offer fishing platforms which, while not always safe and comfortable, are often very productive.

The tidal rips and breaking waves tend to wash this food out from among the rocks and offer easy pickings.

The list of fish caught from jetties and breakwaters in northern waters includes striped bass, bluefish, weakfish, fluke or summer flounder, winter flounder, blackfish or tautog, mackerel, kingfish or northern whiting and porgies.

In southern waters you can catch tarpon, snook, bluefish, channel bass or redfish, sea trout, Spanish mackerel, jack crevallé, pompanno, barracuda, ladyfish, snappers, croakers, grunts, sheepshead grouper, jewfish, sharks and many others.

Many of these fish will be found right near the rocks of the jetty or breakwater and long casts are not needed too often when jetty fishing. However, there are times when fish will feed in deeper water offshore and then a long cast from the end of a jetty may reach them.

When studying a jetty or breakwater for good fishing spots watch the action of the waves. Striped bass will usually be found near the end or along the sides of the jetty where the water turns white. Look for sand bars or deep holes near the jetty which can be reached with a cast. The rips and swirling currents near the end of a jetty are always worth a try since small bait fish get trapped in such waters.

Breakwaters or jetties which are situated in front of inlets are very good spots to fish, especially on the outgoing tide. Here the fast water creates a rip and small fish are often helpless in the turmoil so that large game fish find them easy to catch.

The best tackle to use from a jetty is usually a surf spinning or conventional surf rod. With these you can cast way out and reel in the lure or rig over the edge of the rocks without getting fouled up. With a shorter rod you will have more trouble clearing the rocks.

Jetties can be fished with bait or artificial lures. Usually daybreak and dusk are the best times to use jigs, spoons, metal squids and plugs. At night you can use rigged eels for striped bass. Plugs are also good for striped bass, weakfish, tarpon and snook at night from jetties.

When bait fishing with a sinker and bottom rig it's best to walk out on the jetty or breakwater and cast out into the deeper water past the breakers.

Fighting a big game fish from a jetty can be dangerous if you don't watch your step. The rocks can be mossy and slippery, especially when their surfaces are at an angle. One wrong step and you can go sliding into the water or hit your head on another rock. A long-handled gaff is a big help in landing a fish near the rocks. Two men are better than one for gaffing fish on a jetty. Ice creepers or other attachments on your feet which help hold on mossy rocks are also a must on slippery jetties.

It's true that jetty or breakwater fishing can be dangerous when the water is rough and the rocks are slippery. But it offers a challenge which many salt-water anglers can't resist. There's never a dull moment and if you land several small fish or a big one from such rockpiles you can be proud of your achievement.

12

TROLLING KNOW-HOW

Trolling looks deceptively simple and easy, but there is much more to it than just running a boat with a lure trailing behind. Like most methods of fishing there are certain skills to master and tricks to learn before you can get consistent results.

Once you learn these, however, trolling becomes one of the best ways to take salt-water game fish. From tiny inland salt-water creeks to 100 miles offshore, trolling produces more game fish day in and day out than any other method, and with less effort and work on the part of the angler.

Trolling is effective because it keeps your lure in the water for long periods, gives it constant action and continually presents it to new fish. When trolling you cover a lot of territory and sooner or later cross the path of single fish or schools of fish. There's also something about a moving boat and its wake which attracts game fish to investigate the commotion.

Actually almost any salt-water rod can be used for trolling if it's the proper length, weight and strength for the fishing being done. Thus, when trolling for small fish in shallow inland waters, many anglers often use spinning outfits or bait-casting rods and reels. Trolling rods, specially built for the purpose, come with light, medium and heavy actions. Most of them have tip sections running from 5 to 6 ft. in length and butts from 12 to 20 in. The reels you use, will, of course, balance the rod and line you use. Light boat reels, surf reels and trolling reels can be used with the lighter rods, but for the heavy trolling big-game rods you may need the largets reels made. See Chapter 1 for details on the various fishing outfits.

Lines used for trolling include linen, braided nylon, braided dacron, monofilament, nylon with a lead core and braided, twisted and solid wire lines. Linen, braided nylon, dacron and monofilament lines are used for most trolling on or near the surface; lead-core nylon and braided and twisted wire lines are used for moderate depths; while solid wire lines are used for deep trolling.

In recent years wire lines have become popular in salt water although they were used for lake-trout trolling in fresh water a long time ago. Braided and twisted wire lines are a little easier to handle but they offer more drag and resistance in the water than the thin-diameter solid wire lines. All wire lines tend to kink and care should be taken when letting line off the reel. The best way to do this is to throw the reel into free spool but leave the click on. Care should also be taken to see that the line is even when you are reeling it back on the reel spool.

The strength of the line used will, of course, depend on the rod, reel and fishing being done. Light outfits call for lines testing from 15 to 45 lbs. Medium outfits use lines from 45- to 72-lb. test, while heavy outfits use fishing lines from 72 lbs. and up.

In trolling near the surface, weights are generally not needed and a reasonable depth can be reached simply by

Most offshore fishing boats do trolling for the larger game fish. Here if you charter a boat you follow the instructions of the captain or mate.

letting out some line. But if you are using lures which revolve or spin and cause the line to twist, a keel can be added above the leader to prevent the twisting. In addition, with any lure, one or more barrel swivels should be used to prevent the line from twisting.

There are on the market various kinds of trolling weights and keels which can be used to prevent line twist and provide weight to send the line deep and keep it there. For light trolling, small clinchers, trolling or keel sinkers will do the trick. Many of these are attached to bead chains which act as swivels. For deep trolling even heavier trolling weights may be needed. These may weigh from a few ounces to several pounds. The weights are usually used with linen, braided nylon or dacron and monofilament lines. Wire lines get down pretty deep without added weight although when trolling in strong currents or very deep water you can also add a weight to the wire line. You can also buy trolling aids, such as planing and gliding devices, which will take a line down deep.

Almost all the lures used in salt-water fishing can be used for trolling, but some are better adapted for this purpose than others. Thus, for bays, sounds, rivers and inlets small jigs, spinners, small spoon and underwater plugs are best. For trolling along beaches or near the shore for stripers, blues and channel bass, such lures as surgical tubes, spoons, jigs, surface and underwater plugs, eelskin and rigged eels are often used. For offshore trolling feather and nylon jigs, strip baits and whole rigged fish are usually used.

Trolling is normally done in two ways. First there is "straight" or "flat" trolling, where the line runs directly from the rod to the lure in a straight line behind the boat.

Second, there is "outrigger" trolling, where long bamboo, metal or glass poles extend outward from the sides of the boat. Some boats also have an outrigger extending vertically in the center of the boat. Outriggers usually have a clothes-pin or some other clipping device which can be lowered and hoisted to the end of the outrigger by means of a pulley system. The fishing line running from the rod is fastened to this and is hoisted up on the end of the outrigger.

Outriggers allow up to four or more lines to be trolled at the same time. They also keep the bait out of the wake of the boat, make it skim or skip attractively along the surface of the water and make it possible to hook more fish such as sailfish or marlin. These fish often slash at the bait, then return to mouth it. The first strike releases the line from the outrigger, throwing slack line on the water. This gives the billfish time to mouth the bait. When the line tightens, the hook is set and the battle is on.

When you are trolling with outriggers you can hold the rod in your hands if you expect a strike or see fish. But most of the time the rod stays in a rod holder. You usually have a few seconds to grab the rod before the line straightens out.

When trolling flat don't point the tip of the rod at the lure behind the boat. Hold it off to one side so that the shock of a strike or a snag can be taken by the line alone. Nor is it a good idea to hold the rod tip pointing in the opposite direction away from the lure. The rod should be held pointing up to one side so that the rod tip can bend to cushion a strike.

Fish hitting a flat trolled lure usually hook themselves. But after that it's up to the angler to control the fish's runs, prevent slack and judge the amount of drag necessary to fight a particular fish. There are now many devices on the market which hold a rod in trolling position, cushion the strike and allow quick removal of the rod.

Trolling offshore is done with good-sized boats which have inboard motors and which are usually chartered craft. Naturally, if you own a boat you should become thoroughly familiar with it and have a working knowledge of navigation and the waters being fished.

Trolling is usually a two-man game. One man handles the boat while the other man or men do the fishing. This is especially true when you are going after big fish such as swordfish or marlin. It's a full-time job handling the boat, making the lures and lines work right, approaching the fish, maneuvering the boat when a fish is hooked and then helping to boat the fish.

Even inland trolling in more protected bays, inlets and

Trolling is becoming more and more popular in salt water with the newer and larger outboard motors providing the power.

rivers is difficult for one man. You have to dodge other boats, hold the rod, run the motor and boat and control the lines.

Whether you are using inboard or outboard motors make sure that they are working smoothly. The slow speeds usually required for trolling demand a motor that is at peak performance.

How much line you let out depends on the depth you want to reach, the fish you are seeking, the location of the trolling, the condition of the water and the lure used.

A short line causes the lure to travel near the surface, while a long line permits it to sink deeper. Some lures work best on short lines, while others require long lines. Certain fish, such as school tuna, albacore and bonito will hit close to a boat and in this case a short line from 15 to 40 ft. long is sufficient. For striped bass a long line is usually needed, especially to get down when the fish are deep (See Chapter 13). In fact, for such fish it is often necessary to have the lure bounce bottom at regular intervals, so you should let out enough line to make this possible. In the beginning you can let the lines out to different lengths behind the boat, but when you get a hit or a fish you can make all the lines the same length. Once you discover the proper length of line for a certain area and fish you can mark it so that you let out the same length each time.

Clear and shallow waters usually call for longer lines than dirtier, murkier waters. When fish are feeding on the surface you can use shorter lines than you would use when they are feeding down deep.

The speed of the boat depends on the lure used, the fish sought, the depth to be reached and the type of waves and currents. The best speed is the one which brings out the proper action of the lure used and results in the most strikes. Feather lures, jigs, strip baits and whole rigged fish are trolled pretty rapidly. Rigged eels, spoons and plugs are usually most effective when trolled slowly. Always test your lure on a short line right next to the boat to see that it is working properly before you let out the line. Sometimes a change of pace—speeding up and then slowing down—will bring a strike.

When trolling rough seas you will often be forced to slow down to ride the seas better. Trolling with the current calls for a faster-moving boat than trolling against the current.

"Blind" trolling is done by just moving the lure behind the boat and covering territory in the hope of getting a strike or fish. If you get action you can circle around and keep trolling the same area. Such trolling is often done en route to offshore grounds in the hope of picking up either game fish or small fish which can be used for bait.

Certain fish, such as bluefish, bonito, albacore, school tuna, king and Spanish mackerel range over a wide area and blind trolling is often done when you are trying to locate them.

On the whole, however, better results are obtained if you can locate certain spots which hold or attract fish. Trolling is best over reefs, banks, sand, rock or mussel bars and wrecks and near breakwaters, jetties, sea walls, piers and bridges. Rips and clashing currents and tides are always good spots to try. Landmarks and shorelines have identifying features which often help to locate good spots within sight of shore.

Always investigate other trolling boats, especially when there are several in one spot. Look for fish swimming or breaking water. If they are chasing bait fish your chances are good that they'll hit a trolled lure. Schools of bait fish swimming or milling around often means that big fish are not far behind or may already be down deep underneath.

After you discover fish, don't head the boat right through the middle of the school. Swing the boat sharply ahead of a school of fish so that your lures will also swing into their view.

You should approach a lone fish by first determining which way it is swimming or facing. Then you can maneuver

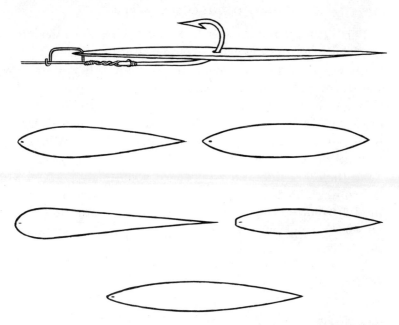

Here are some of the different shapes of strips cut from fish and often used for bait in trolling. The safety-pin catch rig above shows how the strips can be hooked.

the boat at a safe distance, allowing the line with the lure to cross in front of the fish. If at the end of the swing the distance between the fish and lure is too great, try throwing the reel into free spool and allowing the lure or bait to drop back.

It's the angler who is alert and active who gets the best results when trolling. Try to hold your rod or be in a position to grab it instantly if you get a strike. And instead of just letting the lure ride behind the boat without action, try jigging it to provide some added variety. This is especially necessary when trolling for such fish as striped bass. When you are using nylon eels or jigs for these fish a short, quick, jigging action will often bring more strikes.

The alert troller also reels in his line at regular intervals to make sure the lure hasn't fouled or isn't covered with grass, seaweed, straw or other debris, Fish will not strike a lure covered with such material.

Don't be afraid to experiment and change lures and depths at which you are trolling. A good idea at the start is to have the lines rigged with different lures. Also try trolling them at different depths. After the first strike or catch the other lines can be changed accordingly.

Trolling also requires a lot of patience, especially when the fish aren't hitting. Slow trolling for hours at a time can be very boring, but it's the anglers who stick it out until the fish start hitting that reap the harvest.

13

CATCHING BIG STRIPED BASS

When a salt-water angler first sets out to catch striped bass he's satisfied with fish of any size. Small or large—it doesn't matter, so long as it's a striper. Then after he's caught some small ones he sets his sights on a bigger striped bass. Even if he is lucky enough to catch a big striper at the start he is somewhat dismayed to find that it isn't always easy to repeat. Big striped bass don't come easy, at least not until you acquire considerable skill and know-how. You also have to concentrate all your efforts and make it your particular business to go after big striped bass.

To catch lunker-sized striped bass you must know the small but important differences and refinements in tackle, lures, bait, techniques and methods which help catch the big ones. These details are not obvious to the novice, but you can be sure the veteran striped-bass fishermen know and use them. This knowledge, together with the skill they have acquired through the years, enables them to reduce the odds when seeking that big "cow" striper.

One of the hardest places to catch a big striper is in the surf. Many surf anglers have fished for many years and have yet to get a big striper in the 30-, 40- or 50-lb. class. Many of these anglers fail to catch big stripers because they are using the wrong lures or baits or are fishing the wrong spots at the wrong time.

Take lures, for example. When it comes to taking big stripers from the surf you can't beat a large plug, especially one of the swimming- or popping-type surface plugs. The emphasis should be on *large* plugs, instead of the midgets, yet you'll find many anglers using tiny plugs, jigs or metal squids. These are great lures for the smaller stripers but they interest the big fish only occasionally.

The wise surf angler always carries an assortment of lures when surf fishing. Big surface and underwater plugs, rigged eels and metal squids or heavy spoons will enable him to meet the changing conditions in the surf.

When big striped bass refuse to take artificials they'll often go for natural baits. A good all-around bait in this respect is sea worms such as bloodworms or sandworms. They'll usually catch their share of smaller stripers and other fish, but there are certain seasons, such as the fall months at Cape Cod, when big stripers go for worms. When seeking big bass use several worms on a hook rather than one worm or a section of it.

Another top bait for big stripers is squid. A whole squid or a large portion fished on the bottom often produces a lunker striper. In the Cape Cod Canal, where big stripers feed on squid during the summer months, a whole squid impaled on a gang of three large 7/0 or 8/0 hooks can be cast and allowed to drift with the current. In the same canal live herring fished late in May or early in June will also take big fish, while at other times live mackerel will do the trick if they can be obtained quickly or kept alive in a tank.

New Jersey and New York surf anglers sometimes take big stripers on skimmer or sea clams, especially after a storm when these clams are washed out of the sand. But in these

Surf anglers like this Cape Cod, Massachusetts, angler often catch big stripers on rigged eels, plugs and natural bait.

states the killing bait during the summer months is calico shedder crab. They're hard to obtain and must be raked out of the sand along beaches, but big stripers will take a whole shedder calico crab when they can't be caught on anything else.

When fished on the bottom big striped bass can also be

caught with such bait fish as butterfish, bunkers or menhaden, mullet, mackerel and eels. If these fish are not too big they can be used whole; the larger ones can be cut into chunks or fillets and used that way.

An important point to remember when fishing for big fish is that they prefer deeper water. A small striper will often come very close to shore or swim over a sand bar covered by only inches of water, but the big babies need more water, so look for them along the drop-offs bordering sand or rock bars, deeper holes, channels, rips and coves. Also, try the ends of jetties and breakwaters. Along sandy beaches they'll come close to shore if the beach slopes sharply and there is plenty of deep water. .

The need of big fish for deep water is also the reason why tides are important when you are surf fishing for larger stripers. If there are shallow spots and sand bars or rocky reefs which are exposed or barely covered, you can be sure the big stripers will avoid such areas at low tide. But when the tide comes in and covers these spots with more water, the big fish will often swim in to feed. Such areas are usually rich in marine life and other foods. Bait fish often take refuge there. So when the tide gets near high and there's enough water for the big stripers, they will want to move in. However, for best results, there should still be some white water breaking on these shallow spots.

On the other hand, don't rule out the low tides if you can cast into spots with fairly deep water. Plenty of big stripers have been taken at the ends of rock jetties and breakwaters at low tide. In these places you usually have plenty of water and a strong rip. The same goes for some of the coves found along rocky shores. If they are fairly deep at low tide the big fish will often remain to feed. Other good spots are rocky points, ledges and reefs with deep water bordering them.

One of the most productive spots for big striped bass is an inlet or river entering the ocean. Bait fish enter and leave such inlets and the strong currents and rips create favorable feeding locations for large stripers. Inlets are usually best during the end of the outgoing tide and the start of the incoming tide.

The surf angler who wants big stripers must also watch the weather and winds carefully for keys to good fishing. Big striped bass may not feed for days when the water is calm or conditions are not right. But just before, during and right after a storm which creates plenty of white water they often become active. They are also easier to fool at such times since they cannot examine a lure too closely in the roily, foamy water.

Finally, if you want to catch big bass in the surf you must be prepared to spend a lot of time fishing at night. Year in and year out the angler who fishes at night catches more big stripers than the guy who fishes mostly during the daytime. Big stripers feed more actively at night and come closer to shore, so you'll find the top-notch surf anglers fishing all night and sleeping during the day. The novice or the lad who likes his sleep knocks himself out in the hot sun. Then when the big stripers move in at dusk or during the night, he's too tired to fish. However, if you must fish during the daytime, the best hours are from daybreak until about 10:00 a.m., when the sun gets too high. Another good period is the two or three hours before sundown.

If you are impatient about catching a big striped bass your best bet is to go after them with a boat, especially one of the chartered boats along the Atlantic Coast which specializes in this fishing. The guides on these boats know their striped-bass fishing and they'll get you a big one much sooner than if you go on your own.

One of the guides who has really astounded striped-bass fishermen with his amazing catches of big fish is Captain Dick Lema, who fishes out of Galilee, Rhode Island, and covers the south shore of the state, especially the area around Charlestown Beach. In one year anglers who chartered his boat caught a total of 731 stripers during the season from May to November. The average weight of the fish caught was 38 lbs. and there were 23 stripers going 50 lbs. or better. The largest fish that year weighed 58 lbs.

Captain Dick Lema's favorite bait is a live eel and most of the big stripers caught from his boat are taken on this "natural." He always takes along a pail of squirming, lively eels. About 6:00 P.M. the boat shoves off and heads down the coast toward Charlestown. When he gets there, Captain Lema fishes the sunken boulders, reefs and other locations which attract big stripers. By using the depth finder on his boat and landmarks on shore he lines up his craft so that it will drift right over the best spots.

The anglers, usually two or three men, then bait up with live eels by hooking them through the lips or the side of the jaw with an 8/0 or 9/0 hook. Captain Lema prefers the Eagle Claw pattern for this fishing. The anglers cast the eels out about 30 or 40 ft. from the side of the boat. As the boat drifts they let out some line so that the eel can swim naturally and head for the bottom. When the eel reaches the bottom it is raised gently so that it doesn't foul the line in the weeds or rocks. Usually the eel swims around quietly and tries to hide somewhere along the bottom. But sometimes there's a sudden flurry or the eel takes off at high speed, and then the angler gets set for a bite. The striper usually engulfs the eel and since it's a live bait he is reluctant to let it go. When the angler feels the line tighten or the fish swimming away he sets the hook sharply.

Want to catch a big striped bass? Try drifting with a live eel at night in Rhode Island waters. This 49-pounder was caught by Dick Lema, shown here. He perfected the method and has caught thousands of big stripers for his customers.

Another type of boat fishing is practiced by Al Urban of Montauk, New York. Urban has earned a reputation for coming back with big stripers when other boats go fishless. I knew Al Urban when he used to fish mostly in the surf around Atlantic Beach, New York. In those days he would go out at night and usually come back with a big striper or two. Then he moved to Montauk, bought a motel and got himself a 22-ft. open skiff and called it the *Duke.* It wasn't long before he was coming back with eye-opening catches of big striped bass.

Al prefers to fish the south shore of Montauk during the spring and summer months. He drifts off the rocky points and reefs during the late afternoon and casts large surface popping and swimming plugs behind the breakers into the white water. He keeps working these until he raises some fish. If the fish swirl at the plugs but don't hit, Al leaves them and then comes back half an hour or so later when they may decide to take the lures.

If the fish still refuse to hit or the water is too clear, as is often the case in the summer, he waits until nighttime and then returns to the spots where the fish showed. Although plugs will often take them at night he gets better results with rigged eels or eelskins.

When the fish cannot be located Al Urban often resorts to trolling with wire lines in the deeper waters off the reefs. Then he finds that the best lures are usually jigs, big spoons, nylon eels and eelskins. The nylon eel is a popular and effective lure at Montauk, where it is trolled deep for big bass. The light blue or yellow-colored nylon eel is preferred and it is often dressed on the hooks with strips of pork rind or natural squid.

During the fall months Al fishes mostly on the north side of Montauk. Such spots as Shagwong, North Bar and Jones Reef are hot around this time. Trolling is usually done here, but at times casting with plugs or other lures is also practiced.

Another boat fisherman who has taken many big stripers is Captain Otto Reut, who has a charter boat at Highlands, New Jersey. He fishes mostly along Sandy Hook and the rest of the coast of New Jersey. His specialty is trolling and he lets out four lines about 150 feet behind the stern. He believes in keeping two lines high and two down deep. He marks his lines so that they are all about the same distance from the boat. He claims four lures working in a small area are more attractive to the fish than single lures spaced far apart.

Captain Reut believes that most trollers fail to catch the big stripers because they don't troll at the right speed. He always regulates his boat speed according to the current. If he is trolling against the current he slows down, and if he is with the current he speeds up a bit. He says that the main thing to watch is the action of the lure. Before letting out the line make sure it is working properly.

Captain Reut's favorite lure, day or night, is a rigged eel, only instead of using a plain eel he feels that an eel rigged with a small metal squid provides better action and takes more big stripers in the daytime. He likes eels from 12 to 15 in. in length.

His second choice is a large swimming plug with a red-and-white finish. Incidentally, although New Jersey trollers use strictly underwater plugs with metal lips on many occasions, they also use surface swimming plugs for trolling underwater. To get these down they must use wire lines or trolling weights.

Captain Reut also uses large spoons which resemble herring or menhaden. So-called bunker spoons are widely used in May, June, October and November along the New Jersey and Long Island coasts. At this time the menhaden or bunkers are migrating in large schools and big stripers feed on them in the rips and over the reefs. Some of these spoons are monstrous affairs, almost a foot long and several inches wide.

Another lure, which was very popular for big stripers along the New Jersey and New York coasts for a time, is the so-called junk lure. This consists of three colored fringed-rubber or plastic skirts mounted one behind another on a beaded chain. The head of the chain is attached to a Jap feather lure. Two other hooks are usually attached to the chain—one in the middle and another at the tail. Then strips of pork rind or fresh squid are impaled on the two hooks. The most effective rubber or plastic skirts for this lure are yellow, orange or light red.

Just what the junk lure is supposed to resemble I'm not sure. Some claim that the stripers take the lure for a small school of sand eels swimming along. At any rate it sometimes takes big stripers when trolled 150 feet behind the boat. The lure must be given action by means of raising and then quickly dropping the rod tip at regular intervals.

The best time to catch big stripers along the New Jersey coast, according to Captain Reut, is during outgoing tide and the time when the tide changes, especially at dusk, during the night and at daybreak.

Another deadly method of taking big stripers from a boat is practiced at Cape Cod, Massachusetts, by the beach-buggy and surf-boat group. They launch 12- or 14-ft. aluminum boats in the surf and head for the offshore bars and holes. Here they troll or cast rigged eels and big plugs by day and night from June to October. When they can get live mackerel they put one of these fish on a hook and let it swim around among the big bass. At the right times, usually during the summer months, some amazing catches of big stripers in the 35- to 65-lb. class are taken by this method. Mackerel weighing about 1½ to 2 lbs. are the best bait for these big stripers. But the first problem is catching the mackerel alive on light spinning rigs with diamond jigs and keeping them in big pails or tubs of water.

Although big striped bass have been caught almost everywhere from Maine to New Jersey, some spots are more productive than others. The first real run of big striped bass usually starts in late May along the New Jersey coast. During this period fish are taken at Sandy Hook and along the beaches farther south. June is a good month for both trollers and surf anglers. September, October and November are also fine months for big bass in New Jersey.

In New York the best spots for trolling are Romer Shoals late in May and early in June and again in October and early November. Other good spots for trolling and surf fishing are the Rockaways, Atlantic Beach and Long Beach from June to October. Montauk Point, at the end of Long Island, is a productive spot in June, September, October and November.

In Rhode Island, big stripers are taken from June to November, but the best time is usually from late August through October. In Rhode Island you can fish the whole south shore from Pt. Judith to Watch Hill, with Charlestown Beach the number-one hot spot. The rocky shores along Narragansett, Jamestown and Newport produce big stripers year after year. Block Island is another great spot for big bass from June to November.

In Massachusetts big striped bass can be taken in the Cape Cod Canal, off Cape Cod itself and around the islands of Cuttyhunk and Martha's Vineyard. The big fish are present in Massachusetts from June to November. Although fishing for big striped bass slows down in many spots along the Atlantic Coast during July and August, these months are often good in Massachusetts, especially on Cape Cod.

But no matter where or when you fish you must remember that fishing for big stripers requires plenty of patience and perseverance. The angler who puts in the time stands a better chance the one who fishes only occasionally or sporadically.

14

FUN WITH SALT-WATER PAN FISH

What is the most popular kind of salt-water fishing? Which type of angling is practiced by most of the people who wet a line in the ocean? Trolling for sailfish in the Gulf Stream is fine sport and makes the headlines. Casting for tarpon in the Florida Keys or the Everglades offers plenty of excitement and if you boat one of these leaping, silver fish you also can take a bow. In northern waters the angler who catches a big striped bass also makes like a hero.

But none of the fish mentioned above attract the great majority of anglers who fish in salt water. When the average angler goes fishing he doesn't have the time, energy or inclination to seek wary, unpredictable glamor fish such as sailfish, tarpon, snook, striped bass and similar species. He wants quick action with a minimum of fuss, preparation and frustration. So day in and day out you'll find most men, women and kids going after the so-called bottom fish.

Salt-water bottom fish are really pan fish like their freshwater cousins, bream or sunfish, crappies, yellow perch and white bass. The salt-water pan fish include porgies, flounders, sea bass, croakers, spot, grunts, snappers and similar species which dwell or feed on or near the bottom. They are usually small or medium in size, although a few, like southern

snappers, may weigh 30 lbs. or more. However, what the
small ones lack in size they make up in numbers. Salt-water
pan fish often literally pave the bottom of the sea.

The fishing tackle usually used for salt-water pan fish is
the so-called boat rod of light or medium weight. The rods
designed for small fish and light sinkers are about 5 ft. in
over-all length and fairly limber. For bigger fish and heavier
sinkers they may be 6 to 7 ft. in over-all length. Almost any
good salt-water reel holding up to 150 or 200 yds. of line can
be used with these rods.

However, more and more anglers seeking salt-water pan
fish are using spinning tackle. Spinning rods and reels in the
light and medium weights are fine for this fishing if the
bottom is free from rocks, coral and other obstructions and
if the water isn't deep enough to require heavy sinkers. Spinning tackle is also used for those salt-water pan fish which
can be caught on lures. You may have to cast some distance
and light spinning lines enable you to sink and work artificial lures better than the heavier conventional boat rods,
reels and lines do.

The basic bottom or deep-sea rig is usually used when fishing on the bottom for pan fish. Chapter 4 describes and illustrates these.

The type and size of the hooks you will use depend on
the fish you are seeking and where you are fishing. Hooks
such as the O'Shaughnessy and Eagle Claw patterns are used
for a wide variety of salt-water pan fish. Other popular hooks
are the Sproat, the Limerick, the Virginia and the Carlisle.
These, of course, come in various sizes, but as a general rule,
you should use small hooks for small fish with tiny mouths
and big hooks for big fish with large mouths. If in doubt
about the pattern and size of hook to use, ask your local
fishing-tackle dealer to recommend the best hooks.

Salt-water pan fish are usually caught on natural baits such

A porgy on a light spinning outfit fights all the way to the top, especially if hooked on an artificial such as a diamond jig.

as clams, crabs, seaworms, shrimp, squid and pieces of cut fish such as mullet or small whole fish such as killies, spearing, sand eels or sardines. You can buy this bait in most fishing-tackle stores or you can try to obtain your own by digging, probing under rocks and in seaweed, or using various nets and traps. (See Chapter 5, which covers most of these baits.)

Many salt-water pan fish can also be caught on artificial lures such as bucktail or feather jigs, spoons, metal squids, diamond jigs and plugs, so it pays to carry an assortment of such lures if you have a spinning or other casting outfit which can cast lures a good distance.

One of the most popular pan fish of the sea is the porgy or scup, found along the Atlantic Coast from Cape Cod to the Carolinas. This deep-bodied, silvery fish is small, running from a half-pound to about 3 or 4 lbs. in weight. They fight hard for their size and you can usually catch them by the bag full. They are normally caught on pieces of clam, seaworms or shrimp fished on the bottom with a sinker. They are most plentiful from May to September and are found over rocks and mussels or oyster beds.

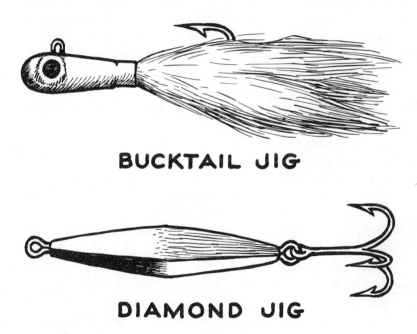

BUCKTAIL JIG

DIAMOND JIG

Two popular and effective lures which can be used when "jigging" for salt-water pan fish.

If you really want to have fun with porgies, try jigging with a small diamond jig and a light spinning outfit. Let the jig down to the bottom under an anchored or drifting boat and work it up and down. If the current is too strong to keep the jig near the bottom try casting it to one side and then let it sink. As it hits bottom give it a sharp yank and then lower it again quickly. If porgies are around it won't be long before your rod will bend and you'll be into a fish. They really go for the shiny chrome-plated diamond jigs. And you can get some big ones this way, too.

Another popular fish which can be caught by drifting in a boat is the summer flounder or fluke. They are also found from Cape Cod to the Carolinas, but they are most numerous from Rhode Island to New Jersey. Fluke are caught on a long 3-ft. leader tied a few inches above the sinker. A long-shanked Carlisle hook on the end is baited with a strip of squid and live fish such as a killie, or a dead spearing or a sand eel. When fluke come in heavy they pave the bottom of bays, inlets and the ocean along the beaches up to a couple of miles offshore. As a boat drifts along the sinker bounces off the bottom and the fluke lying there chase the rig and grab the bait. Most fluke average about a pound or two in weight. But big door mats going up to 15 lbs. or more are sometimes caught. The fluke or summer flounder can be called a "pan fish" because there is no better fish for eating when filleted and fried.

Other fish caught in northern waters by bottom fishermen are sea bass and blackfish or tautog. Both of these fish are found around sunken wrecks and rocks and over mussel and oyster bottoms. Sea bass can be caught on clam or squid bait. Blackfish will also take clams as well as seaworms and fiddler or green crabs. When you fish for blackfish bring along plenty of rigs, hooks and sinkers, for these fish are found around rocks and you'll lose plenty of rigs when angling for them. For best results blackfish should be fished from an anchored boat. Two anchors are better than one for holding the boat steady over the spot being fished.

Those who fish in southern waters around Florida and in the Gulf of Mexico are fortunate because they have different kinds of pan fish to choose among. The prolific and ever-present grunt is one example. It does not grow very big, averaging about a pound or less in weight, but large catches are made and most of them make good eating. To get the most sport from this small fish use the lightest tackle possible. Small No. 1 or 1/0 hooks are best for grunts. The hooks should be baited with bits of shrimp, crab, clam or pieces of fish. The types of grunt you'll usually catch include the margate, gray grunt, blue-striped grunt, white grunt, French grunt, black margate, porkfish and pigfish.

Then there are the crafty snappers, which, on many occasions, offer a challenge to any angler. In fact, when it comes to wariness, the snappers, especially the mangrove snapper, often makes such fish as sea trout, snook and tarpon seem dumb by comparison. In clear water around many parts of Florida you can watch snappers swimming around by the hundreds. But just try to hook and catch them! It's not always easy—in fact, in some places where the water is very clear and they are fished hard, it's almost impossible. Time and again I've thrown shrimp, pieces of mullet and small fish into the water and watched the snappers grab these tidbits without hesitation. Then I would use the same bait on a hook and they wouldn't even look at it.

If you fish for mangrove snappers in clear water use light nylon leaders and small hooks. Use live baits such as shrimp, crabs or small fish in preference to dead ones such as frozen shrimp or cut mullet. If possible try to fish without a sinker

She's holding a fluke or summer flounder over a mess of porgies. Both fish are popular with anglers seeking salt-water pan fish.

and let your boat drift or float along naturally. This can be done in shallow water where the tide isn't too strong. Of course, more remote areas and murky waters often make it possible to catch mangrove snappers with less difficulty. Also they'll at times strike lures such as small plugs, spoons and bucktail jigs if cast around rocks, coral reefs and mangrove tree roots.

The mangrove snapper isn't the only one you'll catch. There are other members of this large family, such as lame snapper, dog snapper, schoolmaster, muttonfish and yellow-tail which will take a live shrimp or cut mullet. And if you go far enough offshore you'll catch the big red snappers around reefs and banks.

Another large family of fish found in warm water is the grouper. They aren't exactly pan fish because some kinds of groupers run to 500 lbs. or more. However, they are often found in warm waters in shallow, inshore spots in smaller sizes ranging from about a pound to several pounds. One of the most common is the red grouper, which is found around Florida and the Gulf of Mexico. The red grouper likes to frequent coral reefs, offshore banks, cuts and inlets. Hooks from 4/0 to 8/0 are used for most of the smaller- and medium-sized groupers. The tackle should be on the stout side; a stiff boat rod, 40- to 50-lb. test line and a good reel will do. Because groupers have the habit of running for a cavern or piece of coral, which can cut your line, you need this stout tackle. You have to hold them back or at least slow them down if you don't want to lose the fish. Groupers will take such bait as shrimp, crab and dead or live fish such as mullet and small grunts or snappers. Some of the groupers you can catch include the Nassau grouper, the rock hind, the black grouper, the yellow grouper and the rock grouper.

Of course, when you are out fishing for salt-water pan fish you can also be set for larger game, such as tarpon, jewfish, amberjack and barracuda in tropical waters. You can use the same rod you use for pan fish, if it is heavy enough. If not, it's a good idea to have a heavier, stronger rod and line rigged up and ready to use. If you see the bigger fish or think they are around, you can cast or troll a lure. Or you can take one of the smaller live fish, like a small snapper or grunt, and hook it through the back and let it swim around. When a big fish, such as an amberjack or barracuda, takes the bait give him time to swallow the small fish before you set the hook.

However, if salt-water pan fish are biting well there will be no need to fish for the larger species. The small pan fish will provide enough sport and fun to satisfy anyone. And when you have caught enough salt-water pan fish you can look forward to some fine eating. These small fish are not called pan fish for nothing. They not only fit the pan but they also fry up to make a mouth-watering dish.

15

HOW TO CATCH CHANNEL BASS

The surf angler heaved his chunk of mullet bait into the ocean and it landed with a splash about 200 feet from shore. Then he backed up the sand beach and put his rod into the rod holder attached below his waist. He didn't wait too long, because a few minutes later something grabbed his bait and took off for Diamond Shoals, way out at sea off Cape Hatteras, North Carolina. The line peeled off the conventional reel at an alarming rate. The angler grew panicky and clamped his thumbs on the revolving spool. The surf rod dipped into a wide arc, then suddenly snapped back as the line parted with a loud crack.

"Did you see that?" the surprised angler shouted as he reeled in the slack line. "Must have been a record drum. I'll bet he would have gone 70 or 80 pounds!" I sympathized with his loss but I couldn't hurt his feelings by telling him how big the fish probably was. Most likely it was a channel bass going somewhere between 20 and 50 lbs. That's the size usually caught from the surf during the spring run in North Carolina. But his real mistake lay in trying to stop the fish's run. Channel bass are stubborn bulldogs and fight like demons from start to finish, no matter where they are found.

If you want to try for them you've got a lot of fishing territory to cover. Channel bass range from Virginia south to the Gulf of Mexico, along the surf and in bays, sounds and rivers. At one time early in the 1900's they were fairly plentiful as far north as New Jersey and a few strays were even caught in New York waters. But today they are scarce in these parts and the best fishing is from Virginia south.

Although the name channel bass is the correct one, this fish is also known by many local names such as redfish, red bass, reef bass, red horse, bar bass, spot tail, beardless drum, red drum, drum and a dozen others. In Florida he's called the redfish and just plain "red." Along the Atlantic Coast he's usually called the red drum or drum.

However, the name "drum" tends to confuse him with his bigger, heavier brother, the black drum. Although they are related there's no comparison in appearance and fight. The black drum is a dark gray hump-backed fish with whiskers below its chin. The channel bass or red drum is a slimmer, more streamlined fish, coppery or bronze along the back and silvery and white along the sides and belly. A sure identification mark is the black spot at the base of the tail. In most fish there are only one or two spots on each side, but others may have more.

The channel bass or redfish is not a true bass but is related to the croaker family, which includes the drums and weakfish. Like most members of this family he can make a "drumming" sound—hence his name.

By any name the channel bass is a favorite with thousands of surf anglers. From Virginia to northern Florida and again in the Gulf of Mexico, the channel bass occupies the same exalted position among surf fish that the striped bass enjoys from Cape Cod to New Jersey. More surf anglers would rather catch a big channel bass in those areas than any other surf fish.

Your chances of catching a big channel bass in the surf are pretty good if you are properly equipped, go fishing at the right time, choose the best spots and know how to use the baits or lures. All this knowledge, of course, comes with experience, but the tips and hints outlined here offer a short cut which, if put to use, will bring results much sooner.

I cannot emphasize too strongly that the proper equipment is very important in channel-bass surf fishing. The combination of sand, surf, tide or current and a big channel bass on the end of the line usually proves too much for a weak rod, reel or too light a line or hook. These fish are real tackle busters and each year hundreds of big ones are lost because of faulty or inadequate equipment.

Two outfits are suitable for catching channel bass in the surf. One is the old favorite: the conventional surf rod and revolving-spool reel. Such a rod should go anywhere from 9 to 11 ft. in over-all length and should be on the medium or heavyweight side. The revolving-spool reel should have a free-spool, a star-drag and hold at least 200 yds. of 36-lb. test braided-nylon or dacron line.

The other outfit is the surf spinning rod and reel, heavy enough to take this type of fishing. That means a surf spinning rod anywhere from 9 to 12 ft. in length with enough strength and backbone to cast sinkers up to 4 or 5 oz. The reel should be a dependable salt-water surf spinning type holding at least 250 or 300 yds. of line. With the rod described above you'll need a monofilament line testing at least 15 lbs. A beginner would be better off with lines testing 20 or 25 lbs.

The heavy tackle recommended above should be used when fishing for big channel bass in heavy surf and with heavy sinkers and large baits. If the fish are running small or the surf is calm you can often use lighter tackle, or if you

North Carolina anglers take many channel bass from the surf.

plan to use lighter sinkers and small baits or artificial lures you can often get away with lighter rods and lines. But whether light or heavy your rod should be fairly long—not under 9 ft. and ideally 10 ft. in over-all length. To make the long casts that are sometimes required and to handle the long leaders on bait rigs, you'll find the longer rods best.

Two types of rigs are usually used to catch channel bass in the surf. The first is the standard three-way–swivel surf rig. On this rig the leader will vary anywhere from 2 to 3 ft. in length. No. 8 or 9 stainless-steel wire is best because of the occasional appearance in the surf of bluefish or sharks. The most popular hook for this fishing is the O'Shaughnessy, in sizes from 5/0 to 9/0. Smaller sizes are used for "puppy" drum up to 15 or 20 lbs., while larger hooks are used for the big 30-, 40- and 50-pounders. A good size for all-around use is a 7/0 hook.

The other surf rig is the fish-finder rig which makes use of a sliding ring. A barrel-swivel acts as a stop so that the sinker won't slide all the way down to the hook. The length of the leader and the patterns of the hooks are the same as those used with the other rig described above. (Both rigs are described more fully and illustrated in Chapter 4.)

The bait usually used for channel bass in the surf is mullet. It is almost always available and makes a good, tough bait which will stay on the hook. Freshly caught mullet is the best, but frozen or iced fish can also be used. Some anglers also use salted mullet, which is very tough and often works well. The mullet should be scaled and if it's a small one, say 5 to 8 in. long, you can use it whole, but if the mullet is a pound or more in weight it can be cut into chunks about 2 in. wide. Or you can fillet the mullet and then cut each fillet in half to make four good-sized baits.

Another good bait is mossbunker or menhaden, especially if it's fresh. It is oily and bloody and draws fish from a distance. Stale bunker is not too good because it is soft and comes off the hook too readily. Even fresh bunker is often tied on a hook with thread or rubber bands to keep it from flying off on a cast. When using bunker you can prepare it in the same way as mullet.

Still another good bait to use in surf fishing is the shedder or peeler crab. However, these are more expensive if bought and also tend to fall off the hook too easily. Hard blue crabs are also used but if you want to use them you should remove the top shell and tie the rest to the hook with thread.

Channel bass in the surf will also take clams, squid, shrimp and chunks of fish such as bluefish, croaker, spot and herring. I've even cut strips from channel bass already caught and used them to catch still more fish.

Although most channel-bass fishing in the surf is done with natural baits on the bottom there are times when they will hit artificial lures, so it pays to carry metal squids, heavy spoons, underwater plugs and jigs, to use when the fish seem in the mood for lures.

The big problem in catching channel bass in the surf is to locate the best fishing spots or the fish themselves. Sometimes, especially in the fall of the year, this may be easy. The fish appear in large schools near shore and the water above the fish looks reddish. At other times channel bass can be seen chasing bait fish in the surf or inlets.

Most of the time, however, you have to study the formation of the beach to locate the best fishing spots. Veteran channel-bass anglers search for sloughs or holes where the fish may be lying or feeding. A slough is found between the beach itself and the outer sand bars. It can usually be spotted by the darker, deeper and smoother water. The incoming waves crash over the outer sand bar, then level off until they reach the beach where they curl over once more. Another good spot is a cut or break in the outer sand bar through which the water enters and leaves. Still other productive areas are inlets which empty into the ocean. Channel bass can also be caught from piers or jetties which jut out into the ocean.

When fishing any of these spots it's a good idea to cast your bait as far as possible. Let it lie there a few minutes, then move it in a few feet. Again, let it lie; then move it. Keep doing this until the bait is almost on the beach. In this way you cover the entire width of the slough or hole. If you get no results in an hour or two you can move to another spot and try there.

In bait fishing it is important to give the channel bass

plenty of time to mouth and swallow the bait. Don't strike when you feel the first pickup or nibbles. Instead, wait until the fish starts moving away with the bait—then come back with the rod tip to set the hook.

Over the years surf anglers seeking these fish have found that the incoming tide is most productive. So, many of them like to get down to the beach at low tide and fish the incoming tide right up to high water. Yet there are times when the best fishing is found in the outgoing tide. So if the incoming tide doesn't produce, try the first two or three hours of the outgoing tide.

Like striped bass, channel bass aren't afraid of a heavy surf and will often feed when there are plenty of breakers crashing on the beach. In fact, some of the best channel-bass fishing takes place when there is a moderate surf. A severe or prolonged storm, such as a northeaster or southwester, however, will usually kill the fishing for a few days, especially if the water turns dirty with seaweed. But immediately after the storm the fishing often gets hot. You can catch channel bass during the day, but the peak periods are around daybreak, dusk and often at night.

If bait fishing fails to produce, try casting a metal squid, heavy spoon or underwater plug in the surf. These lures are especially good when schools of channel bass are seen lying or feeding near the surface.

Along the Atlantic Coast there are two main periods when you can catch big channel bass in the surf. These are during the spring run in April and May and in the fall during October and November. Sometimes the fishing lasts into December. At this time many of the beaches from Virginia south to northern Florida may produce, but North Carolina from Nag's Head south to Topsail Inlet offers the most consistent sport. The most outstanding spot of all is the point at

Cape Hatteras, where big fish are taken each spring and fall.

Almost as exciting as surf fishing is casting from a boat for big channel bass. The procedure here is for the captain of the boat to wait until he sees a school of channel bass swimming near the surface. Then he maneuvers the boat alongside the fish and two or three anglers cast metal squids, heavy spoons, jigs or underwater plugs at the fish. It is important not to cast into the middle of the school or the fish will be spooked. The idea is to cast ahead of the leading fish or beyond the main body of fish and reel through it. If two or three anglers hook fish at the same time, as often happens, there will be plenty of fun and excitement.

Instead of casting for the fish you can also try trolling on the outside of the school with big spoons or feather lures. However, in calm, clear water this tends to frighten the fish so trolling is best when the water is rough or choppy and the fish are feeding over shoals or sand bars. Boat fishing for big channel bass is usually practiced at Oregon Inlet, Hatteras Inlet and near other inlets or spots where schools gather to feed or migrate. This tendency to gather occurs during the spring and fall months. For this fishing, you can charter boats together with the necessary tackle for casting or trolling.

Another form of boat fishing is practiced off Cape Charles, Virginia, during the summer months. In this case the fishing is done at the mouth of the Chesapeake Bay on the bottom, with a sinker and in water anywhere from 50 to 100 ft. deep. The hook is usually baited with a chunk or strip of bunker, but other fish, such as mullet, croaker and spot, can also be used. The fish often run big here, with quite a few in the 50- to 65-lb. class taken during June, July, August and September. So the tackle should be fairly heavy—a boat rod or trolling rod and lines testing from 36 to 50 lbs. will do the trick. The present rod-and-reel–record channel bass was taken

For light-tackle thrills catch a channel bass on a spinning outfit like this one used by Mrs. John B. Swift in the Florida Keys.

in these waters: an 83-pounder caught by Zack Waters on August 5, 1949.

When we move down to Florida we find that it is only necessary or worthwhile to fish for channel bass in North Carolina style, that is with regular surf tackle, only in the surf from Fernandina Beach at the Georgia line down to around Vero Beach. This is because you often have to make long casts, use heavy sinkers and baits and may hook only an occasional channel bass in the 40-lb. class. In the rest of the state the reds run mostly from 3 to 20 lbs. A channel bass in the 30-lb. class is a whopper in most parts of Florida.

For this southern fishing I like a light salt-water spinning outfit which can be cast with one hand. A sturdy fresh-water spin reel or a light salt-water model matches this rod and is loaded with 8-lb. test line. With such an outfit you can cast the small lures used for channel bass in Florida waters. One of the best is a small yellow or white bucktail or nylon jig. Jigs are killers because they can be worked to resemble a shrimp, a favorite channel-bass food in the South. To do this you reel slowly and jerk the rod tip at regular intervals to give the jig the darting, hesitant stop-and-go movement of a live shrimp.

Other good lures for channel bass in Florida waters are small spoons, metal squids and underwater plugs. At times the bass will also come up and sock a small surface plug of the torpedo or popper type. Whichever lure you use, the thing to remember is that most of the time Mr. Redfish is a slow, methodical bottom feeder. He hasn't got the speed of a barracuda and prefers to take lures that are moving slowly. So lures that are worked at a snail's pace and especially near the bottom get the most strikes from channel bass.

Channel bass are also taken by the thousands with natural baits in Florida waters. They'll take small pieces of mullet, menhaden, crabs and shrimp. One of the best baits is a live shrimp fished either with a free line and no sinker or on the bottom with lead. The best hook sizes to use are Nos. 1/0, 2/0 or 3/0—small enough so that you don't miss the smaller fish that hit.

In Florida you can catch bass in the surf and from piers,

docks, jetties, boats and the shore. The mouths of inlets and rivers themselves are always good places to try. During the winter months channel bass often move up the rivers right into brackish or fresh water. They also feed over sand bars, oyster and other shellfish beds and along the edges of channels. Channel bass can be caught in Florida waters all year round, but peak fishing usually takes place in the fall, winter and spring.

Channel bass can also be caught along the beaches and in the bays, sounds and passes in Alabama, Mississippi, Louisiana and Texas with methods and tackle similar to those used farther north. However, in these areas channel bass are also stalked on the flats by fishermen wading in knee-deep water. This is similar to bonefishing in the Florida Keys, where you first locate a fish before you cast. This method calls for plenty of patience and quiet footwork. In these shallow waters the reds are skittish and you have to be careful not to spook them. Any splashing or sudden movements will frighten them and they'll take off.

The tackle preferred in this type of fishing is a 6-ft. bait-casting rod with bait-casting reel and a 12- or 14-lb.–test braided or monofilament line. The so-called popping rods of this type are very popular. (See Chapter 1 for more details on such a rod.) However, light salt-water spinning outfits will also work fine. The most productive lure is a small nickel or silver spoon with a bucktail or feather, but at times the fish will also take jigs and small surface plugs.

Once you spot a school or an individual fish you should wait until you can get within casting distance. Then it's best to cast 3 or 4 feet ahead of the fish—not right at them. One exciting feature of this type of fishing is that you can often see the fish chase the lure. So you can delay your strike a second or two to make sure the channel bass has the lure in his mouth.

No matter where you catch him you soon develop a healthy respect for the fighting power and stamina of a channel bass. From the small "rats" up to the big "bulls" the reds rarely give up without first doing their best to smash your tackle. And they often succeed, especially with anglers who get buck fever or try to horse these stubborn mules. The angler who takes it easy and lets the fish run when he wants to lands the most and the biggest channel bass.

When you do catch channel bass, save those under 15 lbs. or so. They make pretty good eating if broiled, baked or made into a fish chowder. The larger fish can be eaten but they're coarser, stringy and have less flavor, so when the fishing for the big ones is good, many anglers keep one or two and let the rest go. After you've battled a big channel bass you can't help but feel that he has earned the right to fight another day.

16

WEAKFISH AND SEA TROUT FISHING

One day I was casting from a big breakwater on Long Island, New York, using a fairly large double-jointed plug. Suddenly I got a hard rap and hooked into a fish which tore off 40 or 50 ft. of line against the fairly tight drag before it was stopped. When I had gained back a few yards it took another run and took off the line I had recovered and a few feet extra. This seesaw battle continued until the fish had made several runs. Finally I worked it close to the rocks and when I saw the fish lying on the surface I realized I had hooked a weakfish. The fish was gaffed and landed and when I weighed it later it went exactly 7 lbs. All during the fight I had been certain I had a striped bass weighting at least 10 or 12 lbs. That's how hard the fish fought. And all this occurred on regular surf tackle, normally used for fish up to 50 lbs. or so.

This has happened to me on several occasions and I know many other anglers who have mistaken the bulldog tactics of the common weakfish for the fight of a striper. In fact, most anglers who have caught both stripers and "weaks" will readily admit that the big weakfish has plenty of endurance. It will usually make several long runs while the striper is noted for only one or two long runs, which are followed by periods of sulking, thrashing around near the surface or short surges. So while the striper is still the most popular fish along the Atlantic Coast, the common northern weakfish runs close behind.

Unfortunately, for a long time the common or northern weakfish has been scarce in many areas from Cape Cod to the Carolinas. They run in cycles, having periods of abundance followed by periods of scarcity. However, even though recently they haven't been as numerous as in the past, they still provide good fishing in many areas from time to time. They are liable to show up anywhere along their range, but the most dependable spots are Narragansett Bay, Long Island Sound along the Connecticut and Long Island shores, Gardiner's Bay, Peconic Bay, Great South Bay, Fire Island Inlet and Jamaica Bay. The numerous inlets and bays in back of Jones Beach and Long Beach, New York, and Barnegat Bay and many other bays and inlets found in New Jersey are also fished for weakfish. And although the common weakfish ranges at times as far south as Florida they are rarely plentiful farther south than Chesapeake Bay.

Although weakfishing is often done from party or charter boats most anglers seeking these fish are the "do-it-yourself" type and go out in their own private boats or rented skiffs. When it comes to tackle they use four kinds of outfits. First, there's the conventional light salt-water rod and reel, such as the so-called weakfish and flounder outfits. Then there's the bait-casting rod and reel of the sort used in fresh-water black-bass fishing. Next there's a light salt-water or fresh-water spinning outfit. And finally, for those who want top sport, there's the fly rod.

All these outfits have their advantages and disadvantages and each is preferred according to the tastes and whims of

*The lower fish is the common or northern weakfish. The
porgy above was caught in the same waters: Peconic Bay on
Long Island, N. Y., a well-known weakfish hot spot.*

the angler. Personally, I find a light salt-water spinning rod
with a small fresh-water or salt-water reel filled with 6- or
8-lb.-test mono line ideal. With such an outfit you can fish
on top or bottom.

For top fishing you'll need some small hooks, such as
sizes No. 1, 2 and 4 in Sproat or Eagle Claw patterns. These
are tied directly to a 3- or 4-ft. nylon leader at the end of
the line. That's the most sporting way to take the weakies—
on top with no sinker or other weight. It's also the most productive way—when weakfish are in the mood.

For this type of fishing you need some grass shrimp for

chum. This presents another problem: getting enough shrimp when you need it. Shrimp have been pretty scarce on many occasions in many areas. Some tackle dealers, bait dealers and boat liveries carry them in season. Or you can try to catch small shrimp with a fine-mesh net or seine in the shallow water of bays. They are most plentiful around eelgrass growth, shorelines of tidal creeks and around pier pilings.

A minimum of two or three quarts of shrimp are required if one or two persons are fishing. If larger groups are fishing then you'll need 4, 5, 6 or more quarts. But because shrimp have been scarce and are expensive, many weakfish anglers resort to substitutes for chum such as boiled rice mixed with sardines, rolled oats, cracked egg shells, clam shells and diced pieces of various kinds of fish. Squid bait and the soft meat of clams can also be cut up into tiny pieces and used. These substitutes work on many occasions, but you can't beat live grass shrimp.

If you rent a boat the livery owner or operator will usually direct you to the best weakfish spots in his area. Or if you have your own boat you can try in the vicinity of other anglers. Don't get too close to them or in their chum line but line up your boat alongside the other craft, about 30 or 40 feet away. The boat shouldn't be allowed to swing with the wind or current, and you may need two anchors to prevent this.

When chumming with grass shrimp you can be liberal in the beginning and throw over a few handfuls. Then, after a few minutes or when the first fish appear, you can cut down and dribble out a few shrimp at a time. This should be done at regular intervals without a break. If the current is fast toss the shrimp upstream or on the side of the boat opposite the direction in which the current is flowing.

Shrimp can be used alive and kicking in a fast current. But if the current is slow, pinch or cripple the shrimp so that they don't scatter too widely or cling to the bottom of the boat.

Besides shrimp you should bring along a few dozen sandworms for bait. These should be hooked through the head and allowed to drift in the chum streak with the tide. Sandworms usually make the best bait in New York and New Jersey waters but you can also use the small grass shrimp themselves. At least two or three of these should be placed on the hook.

To fish the baits properly you must allow them to drift naturally with the tide, at times as far as 150 or 200 feet behind the boat. Then you can reel the bait in and repeat the process. If weakfish are in the chum streak they will face the boat to grab the small shrimp as they drift down. Your bait should appear as simply another tidbit to be inhaled along with the shrimp.

Most of the time when chum fishing for weaks you can get away without using any sinker or weight, but there will be times when the current is too strong and it will be necessary to place a clincher sinker or a couple of split-shot on the leader ahead of the hook. If, on the other hand, the tide is slow or almost slack, a float can be added 3 feet or so above the hook to keep the bait from sinking under the boat.

If chumming doesn't produce or if you have no chum along, you can often catch weakfish on the bottom. In this case you use a high-hook rig, which consists of a hook, about size 1/0 or 2/0, tied on a 3-ft. leader. This in turn is tied to the fishing line about 2 or 3 feet above the sinker. (See Chapter 4 on rigs.) For bait you can use sandworms, bloodworms or strips of squid. When doing such bottom fishing it's a good idea to use a sinker just heavy enough to hold bottom but light enough to move when the rod is lifted. In this way you can let the rig bounce on the bottom so that it moves away from the boat with the tide.

The only bad feature about bottom fishing for weaks is that you also catch porgies, sea robins, blackfish, kingfish and pests such as dogfish and crabs. However, with the weakfish scarce or not biting on some days, other fish, like porgies, blackfish or kingfish, can often save the day by providing some sport and fun. Big, grandpappy porgies running up to 2 and 3 lbs. are common in Peconic Bay on Long Island, New York, during May and June and they put up a good scrap on light tackle. Many anglers fish for them with hooks tied low or use a combination rig with one high hook for weaks and one low for porgies. Porgies like seaworms best, but they will also take clams and squid.

For weakfish on the bottom if anchoring doesn't pay off you can lift the anchor and try drifting with the tide or wind. This way you cover more ground and often locate the weaks. When you do locate a spot you can drift over it several times or anchor and fish it.

Weakfish can also be caught from the surf in many areas along their range from Cape Cod to the Carolinas. I recall many wonderful mornings in late May, June and July when we used to take some big weakfish off the breakwaters at Breezy Point (Rockaway Pt.) and at Atlantic Beach (Silver Point) on Long Island, New York. We'd go out in the evening or early morning and catch the last of the outgoing tide or the start of the incoming. We'd cast light metal squids with long strips of pork rind or various kinds of small underwater plugs. Sometimes the weakfish could be seen breaking on top, but most of the time they didn't show. Every so often one of the surf rods would dip and an angler would be tied into a fish. After the fish was subdued, one of us would grab

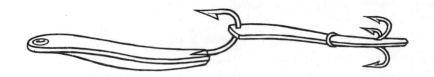

A metal squid with pork rind and treble hook, used to catch northern weakfish in the surf.

a long-handled gaff and bring the fish up on the rocks. It would usually be a good-sized tide-running weak going anywhere from 4 to 10 or 11 lbs.

On moonlit nights we would often fish most of the night, casting small underwater plugs for big weaks. The deeper water around the ends of jetties and breakwaters usually produced best, but there were times when the fish ran along the beach and we'd hook them while casting for striped bass in the white water. Some of the boys would bait fish on the bottom from the beach using squid or sandworms for bait. Shedder crabs and pieces of cut fish such as mullet, menhaden and mackerel were also used. Surf fishing for weakfish is usually best from May to October. The change of tide at high or low water is a good time to fish for them.

In the old days we used to break our backs casting small fresh-water plugs for big weaks in the surf. Nowadays, with spinning tackle it's much easier to cast such light lures. And, of course, light lines and limber rods make it more sporting. Not only that, but you actually lose fewer fish with the more limber rods.

When it comes to fighting Mr. Weakfish is far from weak, and if he's got any size his runs will equal those of any fish found in the surf. The "weakness" lies in his jaws or mouth structure and a hook tears out very easily. So don't forget to use a net or gaff on any weakfish over a pound in weight.

The other weakfish which is popular in southern waters is the spotted weakfish, better known as the sea trout and also called the speckled weakfish. Although they sometimes stray as far north as New York, spotted weakfish are most common from Virginia to Texas. They are very plentiful in Florida waters and along the Gulf Coast as far south as Mexico. In these southern waters they are often caught the year round, although the spring and fall months offer peak fishing. In North Carolina, South Carolina and Georgia sea trout are often taken during the winter months from November to January.

These southern weakfish are most plentiful in rivers, inlets, bays and flats. They are also found in the surf along the sand beaches. Anglers fishing from the shore and piers or bridges often take them in large numbers.

For sea trout you can use the same tackle that is used for the northern weakfish: a light salt-water spinning rod and reel, a bait-casting rod and reel or a fly-fishing outfit. Anglers in the Gulf of Mexico, especially off Texas, use the "popping"-type bait-casting rod with reel to match. On the other hand, most Florida anglers prefer the light salt-water spinning rod and reel. This is usually filled with 8- or 10-lb.–test monofilament line and can be used to cast lures or bait.

One of the best ways to catch sea trout is to wade the flats or shallow waters of rivers, inlets and tidal creeks and cast lures. This is often done in the Indian River in Florida and in other shallow waters in that state. The best lures for this type of fishing are usually surface plugs such as poppers, wounded minnows and torpedo types. These surface lures are ususally worked fairly fast with plenty of noise, splash and commotion. On many occasions, you can also use underwater plugs, jigs and spoons. These are most productive at

These Florida anglers hold a string of southern weakfish or sea trout. They are very plentiful on both coasts of that state as well as in the Gulf of Mexico.

daybreak, dusk or during the night. Surface plugs on the other hand work best when the water is fairly calm and there isn't too strong a wind. On rough, windy days when the water is roiled the fishing is often poor. Likewise, a cold snap which is severe and long-lasting may send the sea trout to deeper water and holes.

If you don't care for wading you can still have a lot of fun fishing for sea trout from a boat. Here the best method usually is to drift with the wind or tide over flats and sand bars. As you move along you cast a plug, spoon or jig and work it back toward the boat.

When sea trout come into the surf along beaches they can also be caught by casting artificial lures such as plugs, spoons, metal squids and jigs.

If artificial lures fail to do the trick you can often catch spotted weakfish on natural baits. One of the top baits for sea trout is a live shrimp hooked through the head or tail and cast out so that it will swim around a few feet below the surface. A cork float or bobber can be used a short distance above the hook. This can often be "popped" or jerked so that it throws a splash which attracts fish to the scene. Anglers often fish at night for sea trout from bridges and piers, using live shrimp and other baits.

Sea trout will also take dead shrimp, shedder or soft crabs, live or dead mullet and pieces of fish such as grunt or snappers cut into sections or strips.

Spotted weakfish usually run in large schools consisting of fish ranging from 1 to 3 lb. in weight. The older and larger weakfish travel in small groups or singly. In some areas most of the weakfish are small, while in other spots some big fish are taken regularly. One big sea-trout spot is Cocoa, Florida, where fish up to 10 or 12 lb. are often caught. The heaviest weakfish ever caught was a 15 lb. 3 oz. fish taken by C. W. Hubbard at Fort Pierce, Florida, on January 13, 1949.

Spotted weakfish make good eating, but they should be cleaned and prepared soon after being caught, especially in hot tropical climes. Like the northern weakfish, sea trout are also tough fighters on the end of a line. The big ones, especially, will make long runs and surges which will provide plenty of thrills for the light-tackle angler.

17

COD AND WHITING—WINTER FAVORITES

If you have never tried codfishing you may well wonder why any angler would leave a warm, comfortable room to venture forth on rough, cold and wintry seas. Yet anglers do go out in the winter, and they are likely to continue doing so. Codfishing has several appeals for salt-water anglers. First, of course, codfish provide the opportunity to do some fishing in the winter. Most other fish have gone south or into the deeper waters along the northern section of the Atlantic Coast. But cod reverse the pattern and move inshore and become plentiful when these other fish are scarce or absent. Also, most bottom fish in northern waters are on the small side, rarely going over 5 lbs., but cod are big and catches over 5 lbs. are the rule rather than the exception. Cod are also fairly easy to catch and they make excellent eating. As a result of these appeals, many salt-water anglers become codfish "regulars," sailing on open party boats at least once a week when the cod are running.

Cod usually run from November to March in Massachusetts, Rhode Island, New York and New Jersey waters. Farther north and in deeper offshore waters you can also catch cod during the summer months, but here we are mainly concerned with winter fishing.

If you'd like to try codfishing you probably have suitable fishing tackle if you do any fishing in salt water. Any strong, fairly stiff boat rod will serve the purpose. Some anglers use surf rods because they like the extra length of the rod tip. This keeps the line away from the boat and handles the long rigs more easily over the rail. Any salt-water reel which matches the rod and holds at least 200 yds. of line can be used for cod.

Today, the most popular line for codfishing is a monofilament nylon line testing 30 or 40 lbs. Linen and braided-nylon lines are sometimes used, but the mono lines are best. They are strong and hold bottom better in the strong tides and currents.

When it comes to rigging for cod I personally prefer to use one hook on a 2-ft. leader tied a few inches above the sinker. But most cod anglers use two hooks, one tied just above the sinker and the other just far enough above the first hook to clear it. If the cod are running small you can use hooks in sizes 6/0 or 7/0. If they are running big, hooks in sizes 8/0 or 9/0 are better. You can use any strong salt-water hook, such as the Sproat, Harrison, O'Shaughnessy or Eagle Claw.

Sinkers of the "bank" and "diamond" shapes are generally used for codfishing. In shallow water and weak tides you can sometimes get away with 6 or 8 oz., but in deeper water and in strong tides you need anywhere from 8 to 12 oz. to hold bottom.

The preferred bait for codfish is the big sea clam or skimmer clam, as it is known. The whole insides of one or two clams are placed on the hook with the point and barb exposed. However, if there are bergalls or cunners around, they will soon clean the hook, so many codfish anglers first put a piece of whelk or conch or a strip of squid on the

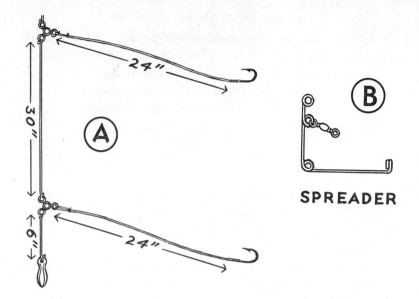

SPREADER

*Codfish anglers use a double-hook rig as illustrated by "A."
They often use spreaders like the one illustrated by "B," instead of a three-way swivel, for attaching the hooks.*

hook. Then they add the clam bait on the same hook to
make a combination bait. The tougher conch or squid lasts
longer on the hook even when the softer clam has been
stolen.

You can also catch cod on chunks or strips of fish such as
mackerel, whiting or silver hake, ling and so on. Small whole
herring and smelt can also be used as bait.

Codfish are usually caught in waters from 30 to 250 ft.
deep. In New York and New Jersey waters, the fishing is
usually done over so-called banks or shallow areas, where
the water is usually from 70 to 125 ft. in depth. Cod are also
found around sunken wrecks, rock bottoms, mussel bottoms
and over kelp beds. Most of the time you have to go well

offshore to find the most productive spots, but in some northern areas and when the cod are plentiful they come close to shore. At such times even surf anglers, jetty anglers, shore anglers and pier fishermen can take them.

Your best bet for a successful codfishing trip is to board one of the party boats which leave from many ports. In New Jersey such boats leave from Brielle and Belmar. In New York they leave from Sheepshead Bay, Canarsie, Freeport, Captree and Montauk. Other boats leave from Rhode Island and Massachusetts sport-fishing ports.

Party-boat captains know the location of the best codfishing spots and head for these areas. If the cod are scattered in a small spot such as around a sunken wreck, the captain may choose to anchor there. While anchored it is often a good idea to chum the cod with empty clam shells which have some meat left on them. Or you can crack the whole clams and throw them overboard to serve as chum.

Whether you are drifting or at anchor it is important to feel or bounce bottom at all times. Cod will sometimes take a bait several feet off the bottom, but best results are usually obtained near the bottom. Cod may grab the bait and then tug the bait or swallow it and move away. In either case you'll usually feel the fish. When you feel the first tug give the fish time to swallow the bait. Then lift the rod sharply to set the hook. On other occasions a cod may swallow a bait and then just lie there without moving. In this case it's hard to detect a bite. That is why many cod anglers raise and lower their rod tips at regular intervals to see if a cod has taken the bait. At the same time, this raising and lowering of the bait tends to attract the cod to the baited hook. And it helps keep the rig on the bottom because you can feel the sinker bounce at regular intervals.

Once a cod is hooked it is rarely lost by having the hook pulled out of its mouth. Usually, the bait is swallowed deep

Many party boats like this one sail from New York and New Jersey ports for whiting and codfish during the late fall and winter months.

and the hook is either solidly imbedded in the tough mouth structure of the cod or lying deep in the stomach. A long hook disgorger is handy to have around. You can easily make one from a piece of wood with a notch on one end.

However, you can lose cod, especially big ones, if you are too anxious. When a cod is first hooked it should be allowed to run or surge a few times until it quiets down. Then you can start reeling it slowly toward the surface. If it tries to dive or surge once more let it go a few feet. Then resume reeling in. If you are fishing from a party boat do not wait until the cod appears on the surface before yelling for the gaff. Do this when you figure the cod is a little more than halfway to the top. If you do, the mate or one of the crew will get to your side just as the cod breaks the surface.

Cod can also be caught by jigging with a diamond jig. Here you use jigs weighing from 4 to 8 oz. depending on the depth and strength of the tide. You lower the jig to the bottom, then raise and lower it quickly. The cod come to investigate and snap at the lure. Some anglers even add a strip of squid or clam to the diamond jig. In general, when you hook a cod on a jig or on bait in shallow water you get a better fight than in deeper water.

You can also catch cod at times by trolling deep—near the bottom—with metal squids, spoons or other shiny lures. Cod are usually taken by mistake by fishermen trolling for striped bass or other game fish. However, you can often troll for cod on purpose if you use weighted or wire lines and spoons. It's a good idea to add a strip of squid to the hook and troll as slowly as possible.

One of the big appeals of codfishing is the size of the fish. Fish running from 5 to 30 lbs. are often taken and fish up to 40 or 50 lbs. are not too rare. You only have to catch one or two big cod to feed a family. If you catch more than that you can feed the neighbors and friends. Or you can stack away cod steaks or fillets in a freezer for future eating. Cod can be fried, baked, broiled or made into a chowder.

But aside from providing some good eating a codfishing trip can be fun and sport. Many anglers hesitate to try this type of fishing because they feel it's too cold to be enjoyable. The whole secret to withstanding the cold is to dress warmly with proper clothing. Nowadays this is a cinch, what with the availability of insulated underwear, boots, windproof jackets and parkas. Add a heavy hat or cap with ear flaps and a good pair of gloves and you will be all set for several hours of cold-weather fishing.

Of course, it's a good idea to pick a day that isn't too cold or windy. Of the two, the wind is the worst spoiler of cod-fishing trips. The cold itself doesn't offer much of a threat, but the wind can make things tough and ruin the fishing. If the wind is too strong from the wrong direction it can create rough seas with big waves. Drift-fishing will be out of the question because the boat will move too fast and you won't be able to reach bottom or stay there long. It may even be tough to hold bottom while at anchor since the boat may move and drag the anchor.

That is why I personally like to fish for cod from a party boat during the winter. If the weather looks good when I get up in the morning I can drive down and board such a boat. If it looks bad or doubtful I can call it off for the day. Sooner or later, if you wait long enough you can pick a day with fine weather and little or no wind. That is the time you can go out and really enjoy codfishing.

Another winter favorite in North Atlantic waters is the silver lake (*Merluccius bilinearis*), better known in New York and New Jersey waters as the whiting. It is also called frostfish, New England hake and winter weakfish. It is a member of the hake family which is closely related to the codfish family.

The silver hake is a slim fish with gray-brown back, silvery-iridescent sides which give off a golden reflection, and a white belly. It has a very large mouth and head with tiny, needlelike teeth on both the upper and lower jaws. If you are familiar with the general shape and outline of the fresh-water fish known as the walleye, you'll have a pretty good idea of what a silver hake looks like.

A big cod like this 30-pounder will give you a good fight. It was taken on one of the Sheepshead Bay, N. Y., boats.

Silver hake or closely related species are found in many parts of the world. They are present in the Pacific and in European waters. The Atlantic species are found mostly in offshore waters from the Grand Banks to the Bahamas. They also range widely in the depth they swim at and they are often found near shore, both on the surface and near the bottom in depths up to 1,800 ft.

The amazing thing about silver hake is their sheer number. They often pave the bottom over vast areas where millions of pounds are caught by both sports and commercial fishermen. They are true "pan fish of the sea"—winter variety —and they are plentiful and easy to catch. Yet, like most salt-water fish, they are subject to cycles of scarcity and abundance. During some years they will be numerous in certain areas; then they will become scarce for several years.

The real season for silver hake in New York, New Jersey

and southern New England usually starts in November and lasts into December and often January. Then it slows down a bit, but party boats fishing in deep water often catch them all winter long. In these waters there's also a spring run in March, April and May. In deeper offshore waters they are sometimes caught as late as June and July. And farther north from Cape Cod to Canada silver hake are often present near shore during the summer months. They are abundant in the Gulf of Maine and the Bay of Fundy during the summer months.

However, most of the fishing for silver hake is done during the winter months, when other species are absent. The fact that they are caught close to shore also makes them popular with salt-water anglers. They can be caught from piers, bulkheads, bridges, breakwaters, jetties and any other location where you can fish in a few feet of water.

For many years one of the favorite spots for silver hake has been the Steeplechase Pier at New York's Coney Island. New Jersey anglers have several private and public piers where they can catch silver hake. One of the best known is the Recreational Fishing Pier at Long Branch, but you have to pay a nominal charge to fish from this pier.

You don't need fancy or special fishing tackle to catch silver hake. In fact, not too long ago many anglers fished for them from piers with handlines, and a few old-timers still use them, although most people now use fishing rods of various types. The most popular is a light salt-water boat rod or medium weight salt-water spinning rod. The reel, of course, should match the rod.

When rigging for silver hake you can use up to three or four hooks on snells or short leaders equally spaced above each other on the line. The best hooks are those with long shanks, such as the Carlisle, Aberdeen or Pacific Bass, mainly

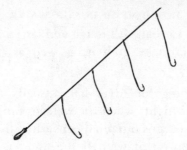

*For whiting or silver hake a multiple-hook rig is often used.
If they are biting well you'll sometimes catch two, three and
even four fish at a time.*

because the silver hake has sharp teeth and often swallows
the bait.

When the silver hake are running small you can use 2/0
or 3/0 hooks. When they are running larger, you can use
4/0 or 5/0 hooks. The weight of the sinker will depend on
the depth of the water and the strength of the tide. If you
are using light spinning tackle, you can often get away with
2 or 3 oz. of lead. Heavier tackle and lines call for 4- or 5-oz.
sinkers.

The best baits for silver hake are spearing or silversides
and sand eels. These two bait fish are often sold by bait
dealers and tackle stores where the whiting are running.
Fish markets may also carry them at times. These bait fish
are usually hooked once—through the eye. (Sand eels can also
be pierced through the eye.) Next the bait is slipped up the
shank of the hook and the point and barb imbedded into
the body near the tail. Large sand eels are often cut in half
before being used.

Almost any large fish like a herring or mackerel, can also
be cut into strips and used for bait. In fact, most anglers
wait until they catch the first silver hake, then cut it up into

strips and use it for bait. It's tough and lasts a long time, and the greedy silver hake grab it, as well as practically any other bait.

The best fishing for silver hake usually takes place on cold, crisp, clear nights when the water is fairly calm. Along the Atlantic Coast this often happens when the wind is from the north, northwest or west. If the water is very rough or dirty it will usually keep the fish in the deeper waters off-shore.

When fishing from a pier, bridge, dock or elevated spot try to pick a location near a light. The light will attract bait fish and they in turn will draw the silver hake, which can often be seen darting around just below the surface. Some anglers bring their own lights and suspend them near the water to draw the bait fish and silver hake.

When the silver hake are present in large numbers you don't have to wait long for a bite. You can feel them take the bait. Most anglers set the hook and reel the fish right in, but many of the more experienced set the hook and let the line remain in the water. Then when they feel another bite they set the hook again. This way they often get 2, 3 or even 4 fish at a time.

On nights when the fish are running well almost every-one can catch a good mess with little trouble. But on certain nights when the fish are scarce or wary, there's one trick which often brings more bites. This is jigging the line up and down in short, rapid lifts of the rod tip to give the bait some movement. Something else you can try is casting the bait some distance away from the other lines in the water. This way you increase your chances of getting strikes. The fish present are more apt to go for your bait if it is not sur-rounded by competition.

The silver hake is not a heavyweight—it usually averages

less than a pound. Some may reach 5 or 6 lbs., but anything around 2 or 3 lbs. is considered a big fish. When hooked they haven't much power or speed to make long runs, and they usually circle around or run off to the side for a few feet. Most anglers haul them in without much ceremony. This is especially true if you fish from a high pier or bridge and use heavy sinkers, but if you get close to the water and use light spinning rods or fly tackle you can have more fun and sport.

In recent years more and more party boats have been sailing during the winter months from New York and New Jersey ports for silver hake, for they are usually more numerous than the cod and easier to catch. But on many trips you'll not only catch the silver hake, but cod, ling and blackfish or tautog as well. In deeper water the silver hake bite in the daytime and run larger than those caught from shore.

On the larger boats you usually have enclosed cabins, snack bars and other comforts which enable you to get away from the cold, but the best way to beat the cold is to dress warmly. Hot drinks also help to warm you up. Of course, when the fish are busy biting without too long a wait in between bites you'll soon forget about the cold. You'll be too occupied with taking them off the hook and baiting up again to pay much attention to the cold.

The nicest part of a silver-hake fishing trip comes later on or the next day when you sit down to eat your catch. Silver hake have a soft, flaky, delicately flavored flesh which is not as dry as cod or haddock. But they should be eaten as soon as possible after being caught. You can fry the small ones whole or cut the larger ones into sections. A silver hake has very few bones after you have removed the backbone. Man! After a day out in the open you can really put away a lot of fish. So eat heartily because you can always catch plenty more of these winter pan fish.

18

DON'T LOSE YOUR FISH

Locating and hooking a fish on a lure or on natural bait is usually the toughest problem in fishing, but after the fish is hooked there's also the important job of boating or landing it. In doing this, experience is the best teacher; the best way to learn how to play and land a fish is by hooking many of them. However, there are some tips and hints which can be studied in advance so that you won't be fumbling and groping in the dark. After all, why take the chance of losing a good-sized fish when you can learn the correct procedure ahead of time?

Playing and boating or landing small fish is often no problem and with a strong line and a stiff rod you can usually merely tighten the drag and reel them in. But when you are fishing with light rods, thin lines and for big fish you must be careful not to strain your tackle. Naturally, broken lines, straightened hooks and even a snapped rod or two are all part of the game and even top-notch anglers encounter them from time to time, but the idea is not to let this happen too often.

When fishing with a spinning outfit you usually use a light line with the right drag setting. This is very important. One way to set the drag is to run your line through the guides on the rod, tie it to a stationary object, such as a pole or a tree, and then start backing up and letting line off the reel spool until you are at least 75 or 100 ft. from the end of the line. Next, you tighten the drag a bit and back up, holding the rod tip high. Keep backing up and tightening the drag until the rod takes its maximum bend. When this happens try backing up again. The line should slip off the spool but not too freely. When fishing for small- or medium-sized fish you can leave this setting, but there are conditions when loosening or tightening the drag will be necessary.

When fishing for fish which, when hooked, start off with long, fast runs, you need a fairly light drag. If a fish tends to take out a lot of line you may even have to loosen the drag still more. When you are fishing from a boat and you hook a big fish on light tackle it may be necessary either to follow the fish to keep it from taking too much line or to regain some line while the fish is resting.

On the other hand, when you have a fish near the boat or shore ready for boating or landing, you often have to tighten the drag a bit in order to bring him in. This is especially true when fishing in a strong tide or current. Of course, you should never tighten the drag so much that no line will come off. With a spinning reel it is often safer to apply pressure to the reel spool with your finger than to tighten the knob which increases the drag tension.

The same principle applies when you are using a conventional rod and reel. When you are fishing for big fish the drag should always be set well below the strength of the line. The longer the runs made by a particular fish, the lighter the drag setting should be. During a fight the rod

The drag on a spinning reel or any reel should be tested at regular intervals to make sure that it hasn't been changed by accident.

should always be held up so that the strain and shock will be taken by the rod tip. Never point the rod at the fish or let it rest on the gunwale of the boat.

The most crucial time in fighting a fish is when it is near the boat or the shore, almost ready for the gaff. Here the angler shouldn't tighten his drag but should be set for a sudden run when the fish sees the boat or the first attempt at gaffing is missed. Gaffing is a job for a man with steady nerves and quick reflexes. Always wait until the fish is near the boat and thoroughly played out. Gaffing a big fish when it is still green is dangerous—you can be pulled overboard. Also, a wild run or leap can break the line.

But playing and boating a fish from a boat is simple compared to the difficulties encountered by the surf angler. When playing fish in the surf you'll find that no two fish act alike. Fish of different species vary in fighting ability and the tactics they use. Even fish of the same species vary in the type of fight they put up. Each fish has to be handled individually, and the surf angler must take into consideration its size, the location being fished, the surf, the current and the strength of his tackle.

The beginning surf fisherman usually tries to land his fish in the shortest time possible. A common fault is the tendency to "freeze" and keep the fish from taking any line. If it's a small fish it can be horsed and yanked out of the water in a short time, but if it's a big one, it will often win by breaking the line or straightening out the hook. Inexperienced anglers have no idea of the power which can be exerted by a big striper or channel bass. I have seen brand-new 45-lb. test lines pop like sewing thread. Large, heavy wire hooks will straighten out or twist with surprising ease. In the old days many a bamboo rod snapped during a fight with a big fish. These days, what with glass surf rods, it doesn't happen so often but almost any rod can be snapped by a clumsy or excited angler.

Even the veteran surf angler often runs into difficulties when fighting fish. Waves, currents, undertow, rocks, and other obstructions combined with the actions of the fish present problems which must be met and solved. And one usually has to work fast and do the right thing at the right time, for one wrong move can mean a lost fish.

The tension of the drag on a surf reel is an important factor when you are fighting a fish—it shouldn't be too light or too heavy. It can also play a vital part in the hooking of your fish. The general idea is to have the drag heavy enough to set the hook in a fish's mouth at the same time allowing the fish to run without putting undue strain on the rod and line.

You can set the drag in the same manner as was described earlier in this chapter (by backing up with your line attached to something). But many experienced surf anglers who do a lot of fishing set the drag merely by pulling the line off the reel and feeling the tension.

The size and species of fish you are after also governs the drag-setting to some extent. I find, for example, that when after fish such as big stripers, big channel bass and bluefish the drag should be fairly heavy, mainly in order to set the big hooks in the fish's mouth, but also to prevent these fish from taking too much line too fast, especially in areas with obstructions around. When using metal squids, underwater plugs and rigged eels the drag should be tighter than when using surface plugs. Fish hooked on a surface plug usually roll and thrash around on top and too tight a drag will cause the line to break or the hooks to straighten out.

When fishing for smaller fish the drag can be lighter unless, of course, you are mainly interested in getting as many fish as possible and horsing them in. When a school of small stripers or blues hit in, some surf anglers using conventional or heavy spinning outfits tighten their drags and horse the fish in so that they can quickly cast out and get another fish on. The only trouble with this is that every so often a big fish mixed in with the small ones grabs the lure—then you have to loosen the drag in a hurry.

If there are weakfish of either the northern or southern varieties around, horsing techniques are out. These fish, with their paper mouths, call for finesse and careful handling.

Many a big tide-running weak has been lost in the surf when played with a heavy hand.

As a general rule, most fish in the surf should be played and allowed to run freely in open waters. About the only exceptions are bluefish, which should always be kept coming. Slack line and trying to be a good sport by allowing the bluefish to run around freely will often cost you a fish. Besides, it takes too long to kill a bluefish if you play him on a light drag. Other exceptions are sharks and rays. With them you can really lean back and fight it out if your tackle is strong enough to take it.

Once the drag on the reel is set it pays not to fool around

Care should be taken when fighting a fish near the boat. An experienced angler like Jack Horing here doesn't try to rush things unless the fish is willing.

with it unless it turns out to be definitely too light or too heavy for the situation at hand, such as when a big fish takes a lot of line out. In this case it can be loosened a bit. When you regain most of your line the drag can be tightened again.

When a fish is hooked in the surf you should feel its weight against the rod tip at all times to avoid slack line. This may not be easy if you hook a big striper. I've had these fish run in toward me soon after being hooked and it seemed like the fish was off. Bluefish will sometimes do this too. When this happens, you should reel as fast as possible to take up the slack line.

Let's say you are fishing an open sandy beach with no obstructions around. When you hook a fish here, you can let him run freely. Usually the fish will head out to sea or run parallel to the beach. If the fish runs too far to the left or right the angler should follow and keep reeling until he's opposite the fish again. The rod tip should be held high, of course, to take the strain off the line. One problem which comes up often in beach fishing in popular areas is interference from nearby anglers. Naturally, if you are fishing with friends you can clarify matters by having an understanding beforehand as to what to do if a fish is hooked. Generally, the best procedure is to let out a yell when a fish is first hooked so that the guy on your left or right can reel in his line.

With strangers it's more difficult. Some guys resent reeling in their lines when fish are obviously present. Others, usually beginners, don't realize what should be done. I once lost one of the biggest stripers I ever hooked because the angler on my right failed to reel in his line until it was too late. This fish hit me close to the beach; then took off at a sharp angle to my right. I yelled for the angler to reel in his line. At first he looked at me without understanding. When the fish was near his line I tried to slow him down with thumb pressure on the reel spool. Finally the angler realized what was up and started to reel in his line. Too late! The fish started off again and my line went slack. I reeled in and found that a treble hook had straightened out. That's one reason why most surf anglers prefer plenty of space between themselves and other anglers.

With striped bass the first run or two is the longest and most powerful. After that, the fish either settles down to short runs and head shaking or bores down. These are routine maneuvers which usually pose no danger unless there are rocks or obstructions nearby. When there are, you have to keep the fish from fouling your line around them or cutting itself off. Often a steady, firm pressure on the fish will make it slow down, stop or change direction.

The most crucial period in fighting a fish arises when he is almost licked and is near the beach. This is where the waves are usually the biggest and the undertow is the strongest. When the seas are rough, even a moderate-sized fish is difficult to land because of the terrific pull in the backwash of a wave. An incoming wave, on the other hand, can assist the angler in landing a fish. There are two important things to remember: the first is to reel in fairly fast when the fish is being swept in by the waves in order to prevent slack and to gain line; the second is to let the fish go out again when the wave recedes. Often the fish can be held in one spot in the backwash, but if he is still strong and the strain on the rod and line is too great it's safer to let him go a few feet. This is especially true when you are using spinning outfits, which have lighter lines.

With a big fish it may be necessary to let him run back and forth several times before finally bringing him in on an incoming wave. The fish should never be dragged against the rush of the undertow.

Finally, one of the waves will deposit the fish high and dry on the sand. A gaff is rarely needed when fishing from a sand beach with a conventional surf outfit. However, when you are using a spinning outfit and the surf is rough, you can save time and even a fish by using a gaff.

A gaff is also needed if you are fishing a sand, rock or mussel bar where you have waded out into the water some distance from shore. Here, without a gaff, you take a chance of getting a hook in your hand if you try to grab an active fish in the water. The alternative is to walk the fish back to shore. This kills too much time and increases the chances of losing the fish. So a small hand gaff of the "pick" or "strike" type should be carried on the belt until it is needed.

When fishing from high rocks, such as those found in Rhode Island, you run into some tricky problems when trying to land a fish. You can't be so high above the water that you must climb a long way down to land the fish. You must choose a sloping rock or find a small quiet cove where a fish can be beached. So before you start casting in such areas find a suitable spot and figure out a plan of action.

When fishing jetties and breakwaters where you must stand high above the water, a long gaff is a must. About the only exception is when the tide is low and the water is calm. Then you can stand on a low rock that is even with the water. Here you can usually work a fish in among the rocks where it can be grabbed. But on high jetties and when the water is rough, a gaff is necessary to save the fish and your own neck. Climbing down among the low rocks to grab a fish or using a short gaff can be suicide if a wave catches you. So, when fishing from jetties, most surf anglers use gaffs at least 6 or 8 ft. in length.

Small fish such as school stripers, blues and others can often be lifted out of the water with a conventional outfit

When the time comes to boat a fish there's no substitute for a cool, steady hand on the gaff. A landing net can also be used for small fish or those that will be released.

or a heavy spinning rod, especially if they are equipped with strong lines and heavy hooks. If you are using a light rod and line or a lure with small thin-wire hooks, a gaff should be used. A gaff or large net is also needed when fishing for weakfish or sea trout.

Wooden jetties present another problem. Here you walk out on a narrow catwalk and fish from a spot where incoming waves hit your legs and a sudden strike or pull by a fish can throw you off balance. It is important not to have your drag too tight when standing on a narrow wooden jetty, otherwise a hit from a big fish can pull you off the structure. If you can get out to the very end of the jetty you can handle a fish more easily, but if the tide is too high or the water is too rough and this can't be done, then you should fish a safe distance from the end and the breaking waves. From this position you can often stop a fish from reaching the end of the jetty by applying pressure on the reel spool with your finger. The idea is not to stop a fish dead in its path, but to let it take line at the slowest rate possible and thus expend its energy. Often, when you do this, the fish may swing away from the jetty and head away from the piles on the extreme end. Then you can let it run more freely. As the fish tires you can start backing up slowly on the jetty until you reach the sand, and then you can jump off and finish the fight from the beach.

The suggestions above will serve as a guide, but in any kind of fishing you can always expect the unexpected. No two fish act alike and each fight is an individual problem which must be handled and solved at the proper moment. The angler who is too anxious and in too big a hurry will lose more fish than the lad who is calm and takes his time. The excitement of hooking and fighting a fish affects most of us and even the veteran angler will sometimes pull a boner in the heat of battle. This is only natural; a slight case of "buck fever" when fighting a fish means that you still get a kick out of fishing. When it comes to salt-water fishing I personally hope I never reach the stage where a fish on the end of my line fails to excite me.

INDEX

209